KU-618-252

'An extraordinary insight into another world . . . He's so shamelessly upfront that you'll soon find yourself hanging on his every word.'

Mirror

'As entertaining as his last two works . . . you would be mad to miss it.'

Publishing News

MAD FRANK'S DIARY

A chronicle of the life of Britain's most notorious villain

Frankie Fraser
with James Morton

Virgin

This paperback edition first published in 2001 by
Virgin Publishing Ltd
Thames Wharf Studios
Rainville Road
London
W6 9HA

First published in hardback in Great Britain in 2000 by
Virgin Publishing Ltd

ISBN 0 7535 0563 0

Typeset by TW Typesetting, Plymouth, Devon
Printed and bound by Mackays of Chatham PLC

Foreword

Francis Davidson Fraser was born on 13 December 1922 near Waterloo in South London, where he grew up. He was the youngest of five children. His father had lived much of his life in Canada, principally near Vancouver, and was half Red Indian. His mother was half Norwegian and half Irish. His father worked for Stuart Surridge, the cricket bat makers, and his mother held three cleaning jobs. It is not clear, but it is possible, that his father served a short sentence for manslaughter in Canada. Neither he nor Fraser's mother had any convictions in this country. Of Fraser's brothers and sisters only Eva, the next youngest in the family, has any criminal convictions.

At that time the London underworld was ruled principally by Darby Sabini from Saffron Hill, Clerkenwell, whose gang also ran the bookmakers' pitches at racecourses, trotting and later greyhound tracks around the country. Aligned against them were the Brummagen Boys led by Billy Kimber. This is confusing because most of them came from the Elephant and Castle. Also with Kimber were Fred Gilbert and George 'Brummy' Sage from Camden Town. The Sabinis could usually rely on the support both of East End Jewish interests and Alf White from King's Cross. There were,

however, other local interests, such as those of the
Wood brothers from Bethnal Green and Arthur Scurry,
known as the King of the Gypsies, from West Ham.

The Sabinis, for whom Fraser worked as a bucket
boy on the racecourses, ruled until approximately 1935
when they ceded some of their interests to Alf White.
They were effectively destroyed as a force in the
Second World War when Darby and Harry Sabini were
interned, although other members of the gang such as
Albert Dimes and Bert Marsh survived. Now, as much
as anyone, the Whites held sway. Meanwhile Jack
Comer – better known as Spot – was making an
impression and in 1947 he and Billy Hill wrested control
from the Whites. Billy Hill's sister, Maggie, was a
high-class shoplifter, a principal of the team known as
the Forty Thieves for whom Fraser's sister also worked.
Spot organised the failed London Airport robbery in
1948, and then a number of his men such as George and
James Wood defected to Billy Hill, who in turn organised two highly successful robberies: the Eastcastle
Street Post Office and the Lincoln's Inn Fields Bullion
raids.

The Spot–Hill alliance lasted until 1954 when, in the
so-called Battle of Frith Street, Dimes, at the behest of
Billy Hill, and Spot fought. Both were acquitted of affray
but Hill then had Fraser and others slash Spot outside
his home near Hyde Park. For this Fraser received
seven years' imprisonment. Spot was effectively finished and Hill went into semi-retirement.

Into the gap stepped for a short period the Nash
brothers from Islington and later the Kray Twins,
Ronnie and Reggie, took over East London. In the South
Charlie Richardson held the reins. Both had interests in
Soho. After his release from prison for the Spot slashing
Fraser teamed up with the Richardsons, setting up
Atlantic Machines, a slot machine company with na-
tionwide interests, supplied by Mafia connections –

Albert Dimes was the London correspondent of Angelo Bruno's Philadelphia family – and financed by Billy Hill. Fraser was again imprisoned, first for five years after the Mr Smith's Club affray in 1955, and he then received ten years consecutively for his part in the so-called Torture Trial. In 1970 he received a further five years, again to be served consecutively, for his part in the Parkhurst prison riot the year before. He lost all his remission and served the full twenty years. During his years in prison he was certified insane on three occasions and spent periods in Cane Hill and Broadmoor.

Throughout his diary entries mention is made of Johnny Carter and the Carter family, also from the Walworth area. At one time the Carters were friendly with the Brindles, one of whom, Jimmy, married Fraser's sister, Eva. In 1941 a quarrel blew up when 'Whippo' Brindle was prosecuted and no money was sent to his wife whilst he served a two-year sentence. It was aggravated in 1943 when the Carters prosecuted the eldest Brindle, 'Tom Thumb', over a fight. This was considered to be completely unacceptable conduct and for the next fifteen years there were sporadic outbreaks of violence between the families. After Eva Fraser married into the family Fraser threw himself into the feud, taking it to new heights of violence.

Fraser has three sons, Frank Jnr, David and Patrick from an early relationship and Francis from his marriage to Doreen. Of the four the youngest, Francis, has no convictions of any kind. The James Fraser referred to is the son of Fraser's brother Jim. For the last ten years Frank Fraser has lived with Marilyn, the daughter of the Great Train Robber, Tommy Wisbey.

Introduction

Sometimes when I'm signing books I'm asked how many people I've killed and I reply that the police say forty and I'm not going to argue with them. One of the people they put down to me I certainly didn't. It was the other way around. The year was 1944 and it was Charlie Gibbs's younger brother, Joey.

What had happened was that there were vaults under the arches at London Bridge station and there was Scotch kept in them. It was going to be good money. Scotch was hard to come by and you could get two quid a bottle for it. People would literally attack you for it. Me and Dickie 'Dido' Frett, Lawrie Piggott and Joey went in after it – three, four in the morning. We were loading it up in this open-backed army lorry we'd got. Someone must have seen us and hollered out or we set off some secret alarm, touched some wire; there were a few about in those days. All of a sudden the coppers were on us. We all piled on the back of the lorry and Joe fell off the tailgate and the police car following ran him over. They set up a sort of road block and the rest of us ploughed through it, got a couple of streets away and were on our toes. We lost the loads of course.

The coppers tried to put it on us and they picked up Lawrie Piggott. I was on the run but Dido didn't hide –

he was more or less at home. Dido was a straight man then. He'd got his ticket from the army and so he could plead innocent when the coppers come round. Plus his mum was a cripple and she said he was with her during the blackout. That did the trick for him. Fortunately the case against Lawrie got thrown out at Tower Bridge in the autumn of that year. Once that happened things died down and I was never charged.

Joey Gibbs's family was very good. They knew the score. They were in a position to say 'You done it and now you're trying to blame innocent people'. If Dick had been on the run from the army as well as me it would have been a different thing altogether.

Lawrie Piggott went bald very young. He did 21 months a bit later and then he just disappeared. I can't have heard of him in fifty years. Jessie Piggott, his brother, was a top man at the jar for a long time and then he jarred the wrong man and came a tumble. He was also a top-class hoister.

Years later Charlie and Teddy Gibbs got away when we had a lorry load of cigarettes in Dunstable. Teddy, who was with a good man Norman Loughran, was driving behind in a straight car when Charlie and I were spotted by police. There was nothing they could do for me and they just drove on. We were picked up on the very outskirts of London and we got as far as Edgware when Teddy went down a cul-de-sac. There was nothing to do but make a scramble for it. We split up; one went one way and the other the other, and I'm pleased to say he made it.

Norman came from a famous family who lived up Kennington Road, a number of good brothers. He was with me when I done Carter in Wandsworth in January 1953. I had a big lump of metal and after I done him the idea was to sling the tool and Norman, who was a red band at the time and used to go round the yard sweeping up, would pop it in the barrow. I slung the tool all right but, as luck would have it, it landed straight at the feet of a screw.

I suppose I was lucky that day with the cigarettes because I'd had a gun and I'd left it in their car down by the passenger seat. It wasn't that I was going to use it on the robbery because we weren't expecting any trouble. There was no thought of a stoppo. After all, we had the keys. It was just if I'd run into Johnny Carter I'd have done him. I was going everywhere with a gun at the time. There's no question, though, but I'd have shot at the coppers, and who can tell what might have happened. Killing a copper was a topping offence in them days.

Constantinople, to ... Istanbul ... Bosphorus ...
... think of it ...

I suppose I have to live with the idea that
because I had ... put ... or ... in the book with ...
the first time ... I ... that I was going to see it
from ... but surely ... we are right now ...
... the days ... when he ... a ship ... that it was
had the ... it was just ... I ... can Johnny had
I have seen that I was going ... where ... with a part
of the time. There ... my question ... death, but I'll ... it
... on why ... not, and try ... tell you ... that there
disappeared ... him ... I ... ... it ... on him ...
until ...

1 January 1984

New Year's always a sad time because it was then Billy Hill died in 1984 in his flat in Moscow Road in Bayswater. Percy Horne, who'd known him all those years ago in Borstal, and who looked after him, was with him. It wasn't unexpected, of course, he'd been ill for some time. The last time I'd seen him was in 1980 at Dorchester when he'd come with my wife, Doreen's, uncle, Georgie Shillingford. That was when he told me he couldn't give up smoking even though the doctors had told him it would kill him. He'd already had a heart attack when he saw me the time before in Chelmsford. He came with his second wife, Gyp, and my nephew, Jimmy, that time.

I remember I first saw him in 1943 in Wandsworth and then I saw him a couple of years later when we were both in Chelmsford. Even then he had star quality. Of course he came from a good school. He was born round Seven Dials and his sister, Maggie, was one of the Forty Thieves, that pre-war gang of shoplifters, mostly from round the Elephant, my sister Eva joined. Maggie was top quality. She was a fine looking woman; very forceful, dominant. I never heard she married officially, but when she was with someone she was right loyal and she could have a temper on her. When Johnny Jackson was having a simple straightener and it looked like he was losing, she had that hat pin of hers straight in the other fellow's eye. She also put the pin in a copper's eye and got four years for it. I've read she only had one eye herself, which may account for why she tried to even things up, but if she did, I never noticed.

Those Forty Thieves were class. There's no denying it and you don't have to take just my word for it. That copper Capstick, who liked to be called Charlie Artful, wrote about them in his book, saying how they just used to descend on a store in the West End and just about clean it out. They also used to go up North to the department stores in Manchester and Leeds. Furs was very fashionable in them days and it was all shopping to order. The trick was to go in mob-handed at lunch-time when the staff was taking their lunch and they'd stuff the furs and even bolts of cloth into specially made bloomers. Then they'd go in relays out to a waiting car because, remember, there wasn't the traffic in Oxford Street and there was no double yellow lines so you could wait as long as you wanted, drop the stuff and go back again. Capstick says that Maggie was the best and that she could get three coats and a bolt of cloth in the time it took another younger girl to pinch a pair of camiknickers.

It's funny how things go round and round. Maggie was great friends with Nell Murphy, who was another of the Forty Thieves and who was Johnny Dobbs's mother. Nell did bird in Holloway with my sister Eva. In turn Johnny Dobbs was the father of the kid by a Nigerian princess who Billy sort of adopted and brought up at the end of his life. Johnny come from Notting Hill originally, and got done for murder with my great friend Jimmy Essex.

Bill had been released the day the Second World War was declared. Everyone who had three months or under was let out in a sort of amnesty. That screw Lawton, who later became the governor who I had so much trouble with in Pentonville and who I later hanged, was furious that people were getting away without their full whack of a sentence. Bill had been doing four years PS. Now he was back again. He wanted to give me his watch when he was released.

I didn't hook up with Bill for some years. He got more bird. I got more bird and in 1946 I come out of Liverpool. I'd done twenty months after me, Spindles Jackson and Charlie Ransford had been nicked coming through Rotherhithe Tunnel after we'd done some clothing coupons at Braintree town hall in Essex. A bundle of clothing coupons was worth a fortune. The job had been a bosh from start to finish. The van had been nicked south of the river and Danny Swain was driving. There was a sort of garden round the town hall and we parked up under some trees, face towards the road for a getaway. We must have touched some alarm although there weren't many of them. And after that trouble under the arches at London Bridge I was always careful. More likely someone saw us. The coppers was on us immediately, but we got away from them and for a time we thought we were safe. It was still blackout and we didn't think anyone had got the number otherwise we'd have ditched the van. As it was they picked us up at Roding Bridge, Barking. Danny was a brilliant driver. He held them at bay all the way and we were hoping to get our side of the water so we could have a row on home territory if we had to. That way we'd know where to go for safety if we got half the chance. As it was we ran out of petrol in Rotherhithe Tunnel. We knew it was happening but by then we'd been hoping to make it to one of those emergency stairways, but no. Dido Frett and Danny got away and I got the bird.

Immediately after I was out I got twelve months for sus. You could get that in those days if you'd had three steps behind you. Just like today with the three strikes rule only not so serious. Then I was out ten days when I got caught with Dodger Davies when we did a smash and grab in Oxford Street and the car wouldn't start so people climbed all over us. 'Incompetent' the judge called us, and said 'Society had nothing to fear' from me – which shows how wrong you can be sometimes. Bill had gone to South Africa by then but when he came back he got three years and we were in Wandsworth again together.

Four of us used to go round the exercise yard. You were supposed to walk in pairs and only talk to that one person, but sometimes the screws weren't as strict and you could sort of close up on the ones in front or lag back, and so very often we made a four. There was Bill, me, Bert Rogers who was the comedian Ted's uncle and who was doing four years for some pussies in Regent Street, and another guy Jackie Sangers who'd been in Chelmsford. He had a name then. Later, when they were both out Bill gave him one, smashed a bottle over his head. I don't know what it was about.

There were some great guys in there at the time. Top men. Alfie Gerard, who did Frank Mitchell (the Mad Axeman) and Ginger Marks, was one. Another was Johnnie Cotton. He was Alfie's brother-in-law. Then there was Jack Rosa from the Elephant who was in for a screwer and who I got to know very well, and George Walkington who later got out of Chelmsford with Alfie Hinds.

I wasn't out five minutes before I was back in again. I'd gone home to Kathleen and the boys in Mason Street off the Old Kent Road and I was up the West End with Patsy Lyons and another guy who'd just won £25,000 on the pools – which was the most you could win those days – when we're nicked over stealing a torch from someone's car. It was ridiculous. This kid wins £25,000 and then goes and nicks a torch, so they say. People in their right minds wouldn't believe it. But the magistrate did and I got another six months.

Bill got out early from his sentence. He'd done quite a bit of his bird by then and he fixed it so Jack Rosa would do a screw and he could jump in to the rescue. Jack pleaded he'd been driven a bit mad because he'd had the cat that morning and so he didn't get any more punishment. Bill got three months off his sentence, while Jack had a nice few quid waiting for him when he came out. Of course, it wasn't a new idea. Bert Marsh of the Sabinis and Bert Wilkins did the same when they were waiting trial for a stabbing at Wandsworth Dogs back in the twenties. They both got off the murder and just had a few months for the manslaughter. The judge then said they'd saved the screw's life.

Bill always said being in prison was unlucky. Not unlucky being in prison as such, but because bad things happened on the outside whilst he was doing his bird. There was his sister Maggie for a start. She died in 1949 when he was doing three years. It was of gallstones. It would be unheard of today. Then his brother, Archie, got caught for just about the first time in his life.[1] In the war Archie had done something like eighteen months' bird for cutting a guy. That was a bit strong because in them days cutting was not the deal it is today. Doughnut Lennie Wallace – he got his name because he liked to make holes in people – cut two Australians to ribbons in the war and he only got six months.

This time Archie had gone to do a job in Manchester and was found wheeling a safe along the road from the post office. He picked up two. When he come out he never did another bit of bird after that, but he didn't have a lot of luck himself. He bought himself a house down in Lancing near the school and his son was killed

---

[1] This is not the Archie Hill who wrote *Cage of Shadows* about his experiences in a mental hospital.

playing on the railway line at the bottom of the garden. Archie died in 1970 during the Parkhurst riot trial. Bill was actually going to come to see the trial but very understandably he didn't. Archie was the very opposite of Bill; didn't look anything like him. He was well built, jocular hail-fellow-well-met and he liked a drink. Bill would have him on jobs sometimes, but in a way he sheltered him. For example he didn't have him on the big Eastcastle job. Archie's job was more laundering the dough.

He had a real set-to one night in Bobbie's Club in Brewer Court with Albert Dimes's brother, Italian Jock, whose real name was Victor. This would be shortly after Babe Mancini got done for murder after a club fight and you'd think they'd have learned their lesson, but they went at it hammer and tongs all tooled up. It all blew over and Billy and Albert didn't let what their brothers did stand in the way of their friendship.

Anyway, before he got out of prison Bill had left a telephone number for me. Jerry Callaghan, from the big family south of the river who owned the Pen Club in Spitalfields, wrote it on a slate and showed it me. I memorised it and I phoned Bill at his place in Camden Town and he said come over. He'd been born near where the Cambridge Theatre is now, but the family had moved to Camden Town when he was a kid. Along with Dido Frett I went to see him. Bill's fantastic. He was still in bed but he got up and went and made tea and then goes over to the mantelpiece and give me £500. It's still dough today but it was a fortune then. I said 'Thanks' and he said 'Forget it'. You didn't have to make a fuss and fawn all over Bill. He just wanted me to be comfortable for a bit and not have to do anything silly in a rush and get more bird. That's always the danger when you come out and aren't prepared. You take a chance on some silly thing and, like as not, get caught.

So from there, off and on, I started working for him. If I'd worked for him full-time I'd have stayed out a lot longer and probably been a lot richer because he'd have made me put money away, but really you had to be a single man. Already I'd got two kids. You had to be with Bill a large part of the day right through until early morning. You'd be in the afternoon spielers, at the races, drinking, watching the card games for him. He was a brilliant card player even though he was hooky if he needed to be. He had special glasses so he could read the numbers on the backs of cards and he could take serious money. Of course, he could handle himself well but it was always good to have someone around to say 'That's enough gentlemen' if a punter tried to cut up rough. Then you might have to go to Glasgow, Manchester; be away for days. Although family life could be tolerant it wasn't to that extent.

Overall Bill was lucky – certainly in later jobs – but he was also a good planner, careful, and that takes a lot of risk out of things so you don't have to rely on luck so much.

By 1950 Bill had already had some good touches including a terrific one in Manchester which the Manchester mob had stuck up for him. They went and did a tie-up of a bookmaker who was fiddling the tax and so couldn't say anything. They cleaned him out.

Bill was a very smart man, not sharp but a classy dresser. He neither stood out or not. You could take him in any company and he wouldn't let you down. He had a fascinating way with him. Look how he had that brief, Patrick Marrinan, in his glove compartment. Bill got him a lovely flat in Barnes. It wasn't as if Marrinan had bird or booze trouble like Sir Noel Dryden, who Eddie Richardson and I had on tap, or the MP who Billy'd got hooked and who saved me from a flogging by asking questions in the Commons. It's just Pat was captivated by Bill; took a lot of chances on his behalf until they got him on a wire-tap and that was the end of him – struck him off. Pat went a bit crooked at the end, pleading and saying how he'd been corrupted by Bill and couldn't he have another chance. They didn't listen, of course, and he went back to Ireland. I heard he'd been killed in a car crash.

By the time I come out of Bedford after that Dunstable hi-jack which went wrong, Bill was doing very well indeed. Harry Meadows may have been running the 21 Club in the West End, all cigars and hostesses, but it was Bill who was drawing the money; and he had another of those big night clubs as well, even if his name wasn't over the door. There were a lot of private parties; cards and otherwise.

By then he'd organised the Eastcastle Street Post Office van robbery of 1952 like a military operation and it was only two years later he had the platinum out of the van in Jockey's Fields just off Lincoln's Inn. After that there was no stopping him.

2 January 1993

The last time the police came to see me over a murder was when that businessman Donald Urquhart got himself killed in Marylebone High Street in a shooting. The guy had been having dinner in this restaurant with his girlfriend and as he came out and was on his way home with his girlfriend to a block of flats where old Bert Wilkins, who was with the Sabinis and the uncle of my friend Joe, had lived, he got shot. A man pulled up on a motorbike and did him twice in the head. Then a bit later that year there was this fellow, Tommy Roche, who'd been working on the M4 down near Heathrow, was shot in a drive-by. Well, I suppose it was really a ride-by in a lay-by – just joking.

I suppose it was a question of rounding up the usual suspects, as they say in *Casablanca*. Marilyn and me were living in Duncan Street in the Angel at the time and they just turned up with a warrant saying they were looking for Charlie. There's searches and searches. If they're really looking they'll tear the floorboards up, unscrew the light fittings, tear the wallpaper off, but this one was really just going through the motions. Someone had put my name up obviously but, of course, they never found any. That was when they said they were from the Murder Squad and were wanting to talk about Urquhart. I told them I'd never heard of him.

As for Tommy Roche, apparently he'd done a bit of work for Urquhart, who'd owned Elstree Golf Club. He'd been a hanger-on of the Twins so I suppose there was reason to think at least I knew him but I didn't. I'd have been older even than Johnny Hilton if I'd done it. I never fancied motorbikes at all and getting on the back of them at the age of seventy was a bit much. I can't remember ever even being on one all my life. The coppers were very pleasant; we had a cup of tea but then they went and took my address book and to this day they've never brought it back. I even had to get a solicitor to ask about it. They said I could go over to their nick in West London but I never did. I might go and get it now I've a bit of time on my hands but it's a bit late; it's easier to print it all out on the computer and I suppose that's what they bank on. That's the trouble with coppers. They can just walk away with things but they don't give them back. It's you who has to put himself about. Anyway, I'm not a believer in going into a nick unless they take you.

They found out later who'd done Urquhart. There had been all sorts of rumours who done it or had it done and why. There was even a report in the papers said it had cost £20,000 but, like quite often's the case, it wasn't drugs as people had thought. It was just a simple business deal which had gone wrong and the loser wanted something done about it. Graeme West, the guy who actually did it, couldn't have advertised himself much better. He boasted about what he'd done. He'd phoned Urquhart's ex-directory number on his mobile and he'd been seen hanging about the golf club. Worst of all he'd left his BMW near Urquhart's flat and it had been clamped and his van had been given a parking ticket near there as well. You can't help the coppers much better than that. It seems right it was £20,000 but no one ever got done for paying West. The Pros said there wasn't enough evidence. According to the papers there was enough candidates though – a solicitor who'd gone to America, a night club owner, someone in Spain, even the Triads. They seem to get the blame quite a bit nowadays. Go down as one of those unsolved cases where everyone in the know can put a name to it.

3 January 1946

It was around this time the Ghost Squad was formed. Scotland Yard thought that crime was getting out of hand after the war and there had to be a clampdown. It was a real good time for us – clothing coupons, cigarettes, tea, sugar, lipstick, anything you name that could be sold was worth nicking. The war was over and people wanted a bit of luxury. Butchers delivered meat themselves in those days and, whilst it may seem unbelievable today, some women would let the butcher have them whilst their husbands was out, for a bit of extra meat on the side, so to speak.

So what Scotland Yard did at first was to have just four junior coppers given a licence to go anywhere they wanted and mix in with the faces and get info about the jobs which was going to go off. They weren't ever accountable to anyone but their immediate superiors and they never had to give evidence. Capstick was to be one of them and that John Gosling was another. They were all supposed to have good knowledge of an area of London. The name was meant to be the Special Duty Squad but no one ever knew it as anything but the Ghost Squad. This 'taking the war to the enemy' was the hand out.

The squad only lasted a few years before there were stories that some of the newer members were getting a bit close to us and that there was a bit of setting up jobs themselves. In fact just the same as it's been ever since. In some ways the Ghost Squad was what led to the firm within a firm; their being unaccountable to the outside just got them into bad habits. Almost from the first Billy Hill had one of them straightened.

Bribing a copper wasn't difficult but it required a bit of care. Really, you had to go through an intermediary. Nine out of ten it would be someone who had had him from the off. Get into them whilst they're young then you could have them like a sleeper. For a few years he might not take a penny but he'd be vulnerable. Then when it was necessary he could be woken up to the fact you had him.

The guy who had him first would be the one to get into him. If you needed help your family would put the word about and there'd be someone who knew someone who knew someone. Coppers would only deal with professionals they could trust. Toe-rags they wouldn't listen to. And there were always professional straighteners about such as Red Faced Tommy. The person who did the business might have to have up to a grand or even two if it was a big job and a couple of grand was big money then. The copper might get upwards of four grand if it was really big and that was four years' wages. Of course, things like bail, or dropping out a conviction to the court was only a score or a pony. When you were done for sus you tried to do a deal with the copper that they wouldn't put you under the Act, which meant a twelve instead of a six months.

If the worst come to the worst you had to go in blind and that could be fatal. I never tried it but there were people who did and they had a result.

In those days coppers never thought they'd be nicked. Take those two at the Bailey in 1945. I don't suppose for a moment they ever thought they'd be convicted. The surprising thing was they were nicked in the first place and the unsurprising thing was they won their appeal. In those days they had a licence. There was no question of saying a copper had fitted you up. Of course the beaks knew what was going on but they couldn't come straight out and say 'I think officer Smith's lying'. Half the time the coppers had something on the beaks anyway. They liked the toms too much; something like that. If you played along instead of steaming into the coppers you might get a bit of help from unexpected quarters. Say the copper said he sees you going along the street touching car door handles. It's no use saying he's a liar because ten to one if he'd nicked you for that you'll have form. What you had to do was go along with him. 'Yes, I agree I was, officer. But I'd been drinking and I was trying to steady myself'. If you ran that sort of story you could get a result from time to time. The beak would say 'I accept the officer's evidence and it's your own fault you're here but I think there's a bit of a doubt'.

It was only later that the magistrates were willing to admit the coppers were as bent as us.

4 January 2000

When I was young no one like us had a bath indoors. Sometimes we'd go to Lambeth Baths, which was quite a little way, and also with seven of us it was expensive. It was also time consuming and you could only go on certain days and boys and girls not at the same time. So, mostly, we had a tin bath in the kitchen in the winter and in the summer we had cold water thrown over us in the yard. In the summer I'd go swimming in the Thames near the Oxo building. My parents insisted we kept ourselves clean. They were both spotless. We may have had snotty noses but we had a real scrub down once a week. Howley Place had a flush lavatory with a wooden seat which didn't lift up and that was in the yard as well.

The first bathroom of my own I ever had was in the 1950s, when I went down to Brighton to make sure Sammy Bellson didn't put up any money for Spot's defence and I stayed in his flat in Marine Parade near where Laurence Olivier lived. Afterwards Doreen, my wife who I met there, bought a house in Hove and, of course, that had a bath but, by then, I was in my thirties.

When I lived with Kathleen and we had the boys we had a flat with a lavatory, which we shared with the other flat on the same landing. There were wooden stairs to the top where we lived and we had a fireplace in the main room. It must have been the biggest fire hazard there was.

Things have changed in the area. Old Lumps and Bumps, who had the flower stall where Buster Edwards later worked, used to put business my way. She got her name because of the beatings she had from the police whilst she was drunk. She was a big woman who never wore underpants and she used to warm her bum before the fire in the pub when it was cold. She just pulled up her skirt and toasted a cheek at a time. No one said a thing. She'd probably have belted them if they had. I remember once she pointed out a car at the back of Waterloo station which looked good. There were three of us and we can't have been more than eleven or twelve. We broke in and there was a briefcase with about a hundred quid in it. A fortune for us. We actually floated a few ten shilling notes in the Thames. Of course we gave Lumps something but we didn't tell her how much we'd got. Afterwards I kept giving my mother ten shilling here, a pound there. I couldn't say I'd found it all in one go. She'd have told my dad and he would have made me hand it in. I wasn't seeing it go to the coppers.

Like so many, my mother used to pop my father's suit on a Monday; blue serge it was. That was my job, well Eva's and mine. Most weeks I would take it to Harvey and Thompson opposite St John's Church near Waterloo Bridge. Everyone had to borrow. We'd get £2 at the most for it and we had to go and pay the interest and collect it on a Friday. Dad never knew. If he put it on at all, he'd only wear it to go out on a Saturday night with Mum to the pub or possibly on a Sunday when he had his lunch. The rest of the time it would be hanging in the cupboard or down the pawnshop.

Nowadays I wake up about six every morning. That's a lay over from being in the nick. There the door would be opened at seven and you'd be slopping out. If you were in the prison hospital you were given pyjamas but you slept on paper sheets. Otherwise you was naked or in your shirt and pants if it was cold. You'd be like winning the pools to get pyjamas. Generally you shaved in your cell but when I was in Norwich there was a recess you could use. The lavatories had half doors so there was no question of two people getting in them at one time for homo business. Not that there was much of that.

Now at home I get up and make a cup of coffee for Marilyn, then if it's a nothing day I take it fairly easy for an hour or so and pop out and get the newspapers. I read the *Sun* and the *Mail* and sometimes the *Telegraph*. If I'm on the underground I see that *Metro*. I got a right slagging off in it over my last book, saying why should ex-cons make money and so on and who wanted to know what they thought. Their readers is an answer for a start, because only the week before they'd had an interview with me about my life in London.

Sometimes I'll have breakfast in a café. I'll eat anything and that's another lay over from prison. You were lucky to get enough food there and if you were picky then you starved. Very often I'll eat out for lunch as well.

I like to take it easy. I watch a lot of telly and those old films in the afternoon. I'm a great Arsenal supporter but I never watch them. I've been to Arsenal matches in the past, of course, but I don't go now. I love them too much. Sometimes I'll listen on the radio and if the ball's in their penalty area I switch off until I think they'll have cleared it. If they've won and they're on *Match of the Day*, I'll watch them then but not if they've lost. I used to go to cup finals if they was in them and, whilst I was away, Doreen always got tickets for our boy Francis from one of the best, Johnny Cohen. He was known as Johnny the Stick, because he had a bit of a limp. He was Stan Flashman, the celebrated tout's boss originally. He used to go to sleep in a Tottenham shirt but he always used to say he made his money out of Arsenal. His word was his bond. If he said he could get you into Buckingham Palace he'd have the tickets in his hand by the time you turned up by the fountain.

Sometimes of an afternoon I'll go up West and see my nephew, Jimmy, in the Tin Pan in Archer Street. It's been redecorated since the days when they hung my prison sweater and slippers over the bar as a tribute. It's a winebar itself now.

I try not to get webbed up, but sometimes I get taken from one club to another. I pay my corner but it gets expensive. The days are gone when we went boozing and then turned up at the Astor and stayed there until five in the morning. Four o'clock would be the very latest nowadays. I find if I drink vodka and lemonade I can drink it all night, but if I start mixing it with light ale then I've got a thick head the next morning. Generally I'm in bed by midnight watching another of the old films. I like those Sergeant Bilko reruns with Phil Silvers. Even now they're hilarious, dated but still good.

I've only ever voted twice in my life and neither time did it do any good. The first was when I was in my early twenties and my brother-in-law, Peggy's husband, was a keen communist. He got me interested and I think for a bit I was even a member of the Young Communists. Then I voted Tory at the last general election and look what good that did.

Of course if I'm doing a talk or a show it's different. Then I get the afternoon train. I do most up in the North where the boxing promoter Mike Dalton has been very good to me. He's arranged loads of shows – dinner, sometimes a stripper, a comedian and then I round off the evening. I do an hour or so and I'll answer questions. Sometimes Marilyn's dad, Tommy Wisbey, comes with me and talks about the train. After the talk I stay and sign any of the books people have brought. That can go on another hour. It's only fair to stick around and not rush off back to the hotel. People have paid good money, the least I can do is be with them.

7 January 2000

The street I live in now, Browning Street is named after the poet. I'm right next door to where he and Elizabeth Barrett lived. You get a lot of people wanting to see where they lived. Opposite's a second-hand furniture and pine-stripping business run by my old pal Mickey, who got hold of Jack the Rat Duval's wig, put jam in it and stuck it back on his head, just before he was going to court to give evidence against us in the Torture Trial. His place is a converted chapel. You can see it from the shape of the windows. Apparently, at the turn of the century there was four churches in the street. Then it would have been just about countryside.

And whilst I didn't live there then, it was here the last time I saw Gus Thatcher. Just on the corner two doors from where I am now. He was a big man, well over six feet, and he'd done a good bit of bird for blagging, and when I saw him he was out on the hostel scheme. I don't know now if he was wanted at the time but within a couple of weeks he was going to get involved in a big case.

The last time I heard of Gus was when I was down the punishment block in Durham prison at the time of the 1979 election. It was the time I was being moved round the country every six or eight weeks. They thought it was the best way of controlling me and I didn't mind because it was a day out, and if I was lucky I could see the countryside as I got driven to the next nick. Then it was straight down the punishment block; not on a charge but the governor could order you down on a general rule of keeping order in the prison. I was allowed my wireless so it wasn't too bad at all. That's when I heard Gus's voice. He was on a debate about capital punishment, and after all he was a good one to have on the wireless because he'd been reprieved.

His real name was George but he was always known as Gus and he'd been on a robbery at the Royal Arsenal Co-op in 1963 in which a lorry driver had been shot by accident. It was the usual raid: in with guns, make the staff lie on the floor and off with the money, which was around £400. Nothing to it and then, just like happened with Joey Martin a few years later, in comes someone and tries to stop it. Off goes the gun and the bloke's dead on the floor. All this happened on 18 November and Gus was picked up about three weeks later along with Charles Connelly, Johnny Hilton and Philip Kelly who turned out to be a right funny one.

The trial was a strange one because from the start Kelly blamed Gus for the actual shooting; the witnesses weren't that sure who'd done what and a prisoner gives evidence and some letters get produced from Kelly which say that he now admitted the shooting. Then Charlie Connelly's wife goes into hospital to have a baby and the judge has to decide whether he can move the trial outside the City of London to go and hear her evidence. Of course, it's crucial evidence because she's giving him an alibi. In the end he decides he can and about fifty of them go off to the hospital and hear the evidence in a special room. The jury was out about four hours before they found Gus guilty of capital murder. In those days the judge would ask if the defendant had anything to say before he passed sentence, and Kelly ups and says it was him who fired the shot.

The judge had laid it on a bit thick when he passed the death sentence saying 'You shot this man brutally and without pity and for that crime the law provides but one sentence, that you too shall die'. In fact the judge was wrong. Gus didn't. The Court of Appeal said there'd been a poor summing-up, reduced the sentence to non-capital murder and give him life. But before that Kelly'd gone and confessed to a priest that he was the one who'd done the shooting. The Court wasn't allowing that evidence though; absolutely inadmissible they said. Personally I think they must have had some doubts about the whole thing though, and that's why they reduced it against Gus. They also said that the judge had been most unfair to Charlie Connelly, and had rubbished his expert witness and not put his defence properly to the jury, and they quashed the non-capital murder conviction. What they did, though, was let the Pros have another go at him on the robbery.

8 January 2000

I see that politician Jonathan Aitken got let out. I don't approve of what was going to be done to him; drug him and then photo him naked with another con and try and sell the film to the papers. That is, if the whole thing wasn't a get up. You can never tell. Someone might just have put the story about to get a gee from it. But if it was true I don't hold with it. It wouldn't have been my scene. If I was that concerned I'd have bashed him up and that would have been that.

I think the only other MP I met in prison was John Stonehouse after he got caught faking his death and he was put in Norwich. He was a very interesting and likeable man. I said he was an idiot. He should have got in touch with someone like me, but he said how did he know anyone like me? He said he wasn't the only government minister who got into mischief. He was the one who was caught. It may have been sour grapes but it didn't seem like it. The mistake I made was getting caught, he'd say. Same as all of us.

By all accounts though Aitken seems to have got on well enough. You never can tell how people are going to do their bird. It depends on the person you are how you cope. I've met many prisoners from all ranks and seen the way it affects them. Some who've had a good education, never been in prison before, they handle it superbly. But many people, many, many others it slaughters them. They come out broken people, lost their spark, everything.

You have to do it a day at a time. Expect nothing and if you get something be grateful for it. It's difficult for me now to say what it's like now because, thank God, I've been out over ten years and there's no doubt prison has improved. Nevertheless, when them gates crash shut, no matter how improved prison has become, it's still prison and they've lost their freedom.

People have no idea. You go in and your clothes are taken. You're strip searched and this is done publicly in the reception; niceties are out of the window. This is the idea; to let you know you're in prison. Your clothes are bagged up; your watch and jewellery taken. They even split my St Christopher medallion at Durham and took it away from me. I got it back before I was released but by then prisoners were allowed things like that. I must have chinned half a dozen screws over that medallion.

Prison authorities are jealous from the screws upwards. They'll try to knock down the educated. On the other hand, most likely they'll eventually give them a decent job, once they've had the delight of knocking the prisoner's ego about.

12 January 2000

I don't know what Freddie Foreman thought he was up to appearing on that television programme about how he killed Frank Mitchell and Ginger Marks, but it did him and his reputation no good whatsoever. Saying sorry to the families; what good did that do? You'd have to be skint to do it and I didn't think he was that skint. I know his wife Maureen took a lot of the dough when she sold the villa in Spain but I didn't know he was that hard up. What did he get? A grand, two grand? Even if he did he's gone and forfeited all the respect everyone's had for him over the years and until now he's been well respected. You wouldn't have got me to do it, not for a million.

I thought in the first programme that they might have filmed the grass Albert Donoghue and Fred separately, but in the second there was the two of them together. There he was on a programme with the man who grassed him up; tried to get him done for murder. What was he thinking? It would be like me appearing on a programme with Bennie Coulson who put us all away in the Richardson trial. In Fred's case it's even worse because you're talking about a murder. Every grass has a story about why they went hooky. I've never heard one say 'I'm a grass and I'm proud of it'. So Donoghue says the Twins wanted him to take the blame for Mitchell. He should have turned round and said 'I'll help you in any way I can but not that'. Reggie phoned me up after the programme. He thinks it's killed off his chance of parole when he goes up in March. He thinks he's guaranteed a knock-back now.

I never knew what Reggie was doing having Donoghue around in the first place. You can't shoot a man, like Reggie shot Donoghue, in the leg and expect him to remain loyal. In them days Donoghue was physically a very dangerous man.

I've known Freddie years. Jerry Callaghan introduced me when his family took that pub in Lant Street. I used to go in a lot; took my mum and dad in once or twice. Fred's always been a cold and calculating man and that 'I've never killed for money' is a load of bollocks. I don't know why he said those things about Charlie Kray being at a meeting when it was decided Frank Mitchell had to go. I've never heard that being mentioned. I don't know why he's turned against poor old Charlie Kray either, saying he was a fence and this at a time when he needs help the most.

Then there's Nipper Read, who did the Krays, saying Freddie could have been a grass all them years ago and was an informant for Frank Williams, who was Tommy Butler's man. Nipper may be putting the mix in but it makes you wonder about something.

I know that Freddie's pub was always full of coppers but there was always a certain amount of drinking together. Now it makes me wonder about Mr Smith's Club. There's always been stories that he set it up as a favour to Reggie and now, after seeing him on telly, I'd believe anything. It was Freddie who arranged the stitching for Billy Hayward when he was cut on the head after he got away from the fight. There's no doubt that Butler elbowed out the superintendent when he was doing me for Dickie Hart's murder and took the case over, leaving him with just the affray. It's things like that.

I wonder what Fred's great friend Micky Regan is thinking. At one time if you saw one of them the other wouldn't be very far behind. Micky came from a big family in Clerkenwell and looked after a lot of clubs round Spitalfields.

I knew him when he was about nineteen. Jimmy Humphreys, Eva's husband, Jimmy, and me had nicked a lorry load of tea from outside what was the Ministry of Health building by the Elephant. It was a big parking site and we had the wire. The driver was gone and so we took it rather than wait and have to do a tie-up. It was going to be big money because shopkeepers would literally bite your hand off for it. The trouble was we didn't have a pull in, so we drove the lorry over to the Italians in Clerkenwell and parked temporarily on a bomb site. We got hold of Battles Rossi and him and little Eddie Anthony finally found us a pull in over in Hackney. The next bit of trouble was that it had been pouring down and we was stuck. We recruited every decent thief in London and Micky Regan,who knew Billy Blythe, come and help us out. We were just selling it off the back of the van. Literally fell off the back of a lorry.

My sister Eva's always wondered about Freddie. Both him and his brother George knew Bennie Coulson well and she's always felt he could have done more to help her when she got nicked for conspiracy to pervert the course of justice. That was a get up if ever there was one and she could have done with a bit of help.

Fred ought to have a new edition of his book out. It could be called Disrespect.

I can't say I've any time at all for Myra Hindley and whether she's got some sort of brain tumour or whether she hasn't. As far as I'm concerned I'd leave her in prison and not go to the expense of taking her to these hospitals for tests. I've no mercy for her at all. I wish I could find mercy but I can't. I think I might just about if when she'd gone all religious, and become a left-hander like me, she'd told the coppers where the other kids' bodies were. That's what I have against her apart from the killings themselves, which is quite enough. She's left their families hanging on for news over all these years when she'd known where they were and she wouldn't say until it suited her. But no she wouldn't and, in my book, that does for her. Shows people are right when they say she's being manipulative.

Over the years a fair number of girls have steamed into her in the nick and Eva was one of the first. It was when Eva got done over that so-called conspiracy to pervert, which was about as unfair a thing as could have happened in 1965. Hindley wasn't long into her sentence by then and Eva did her in Holloway. She lost a bit of remission over it but she thought it was well worth it. Janie Jones, the girl who got that bird for running prostitutes after the copper Bert Wickstead did her, done Hindley in the seventies. That funny girl Josie O'Dwyer was another one.

Josie was a lez who'd said a council worker from Highbury had tried to rape her and she'd killed him in self-defence. Then at her trial she changed her mind and jumped up shouting she was going to plead guilty. Stupid thing to do. Nowadays she'd have more than half a chance with that sort of defence. More than that, she had an epileptic fit during the trial and so she'd have had the jury on her side. She got life, of course, and I heard she topped herself in the nick a couple of years back. Pity Myra Hindley didn't do so years back.[1]

Funnily, I was never in the nick with either Ian Brady or Peter Sutcliffe. You'd think that over the years I'd have run into them once but, there again, perhaps the authorities were keeping us deliberately apart because I'd have done Brady for sure, as poor old Jackie O'Connell would have said.

I remember hearing that tape the Ripper was supposed to have sent to the coppers. The one that turned out to be a fake. The one who spoke had a Geordie accent and I could have sworn it was a screw I chinned in my cell at Norwich in 1977. Of course it wasn't but the accent was identical. The other screws came to his rescue, pulled him out and banged me up, but one of them left his hat on the floor. They pleaded with me to give it back, even the badge because if he had that he could get a new one from the authorities, but I just laughed at them. I pissed in the hat and gave it them but I kept the badge. They could have steamed in and got it back but their arseholes went and they swallowed it. I was nicked for assault, of course.

---

[1] On 11 October 1995 39-year-old Josie O'Dwyer was charged with the murder of 39-year-old Peter Sutherland. On 10 February 1996 she changed her plea to guilty. The prosecution had alleged she had struck him nine blows on the head, some from behind. She had claimed that whilst in her flat in Pyrland Road, Islington, he had lunged at her breast saying that what she needed was a good man.

15 January 2000

I took a coach party out today for a kid's twenty-first birthday. I do it quite regular. Marilyn drives, gives them a song at the wheel and I tell them what life's been like. It's funny how it came about. It was an accident, really. I was on this programme on Talk Radio with George Best, the footballer, and I came over so good Richard Littlejohn rang me up and got me on some of his shows. But that's by the by; it was the guy from Talk Radio suggested the idea of doing tours of the East End. He got in touch with that tour company Evan Evans and they put me in their programme – the picture was opposite a tour round Buckingham Palace – everyone met me just off Russell Square. They provided the driver but I had to give him a drink and, by the time it all worked out, our whack didn't come to much. Also they wanted it twice a week and, to be frank, at 35 in a coach there wasn't that demand out of season. So I started doing it on my own. Put it on my website and I do a steady trade. We rent a minivan from down the road and I'll do a tour at the weekend or any day anyone wants. Thirty quid a head a time, dirt cheap really for a four-hour tour.

They come to Browning Street and we start off at Charlie and Eddie Richardson's yard, then we go to where Marilyn lived and where the Train Robbery was planned. Then we go to where Mr Smith's Club was – that's been pulled down long ago – and then to Waterloo where I was born. After that it's over the water to the Turnmills where I got shot and I show them Little Italy where the Sabinis come from. Then we go to Repton Boxing Club and they get in the ring with me, and round the corner is where Reggie got married to Frances Shea. I show them where Vallance Road is and Evering Road where Jack the Hat copped it and, of course, the Blind Beggar and the Grave Maurice, which is just a bit further along the Mile End Road, where they get a drink and a bit of a fuss made of them. They make a fuss of me in there as well. Then it's the Gun pub in Spitalfields near where the Eastcastle Street Robbery money got hid by Sonny Sullivan for Billy Hill; the Old Bailey and home. Of course there's plenty of time to have their photos taken where they want and most people bring their books to sign as well.

If they want a drink with us after that's well and good but they don't have to. These kids were great and we didn't get home till four in the morning. We get all sorts on the tour and from all over the place. I remember there was one old couple come up from Bath when I was doing it with the company. They had to get up early because it was a quick start in the morning to avoid the traffic. They enjoyed it so much they come back a fortnight later and do it all over again.

19 January 2000

It's just about seven years since Michael Sams kidnapped Stephanie Slater, that young estate agent out of Perry Barr, Birmingham, and held her captive in a box for eight days so she couldn't recognise him. He pretended he wanted to buy a house and he grabbed her when he went there to look it over. The previous year he'd killed another young girl, Julie Dart, a brass from Leeds. He'd hit her over the head and her body was found in a field in Lincolnshire. This time he'd tried to blag £200,000 off British Rail, saying he'd derail a train if he didn't get the money.

This Stephanie did well; she was a courageous kid. She got him talking and it's well known that the longer you keep someone talking to you the less likely it is at the end of the day they'll do you any harm. It's like those hostage situations they had in Stockholm and other places in the 1970s. By the end of one of them, one of the women was in love with her captor and was in the club by him. Anyway Stephanie Slater gets him talking and learns what she can about him. Eventually it worked. Under instructions from the coppers her employer paid over £175,000. So far as I read, the money was to be placed on a tray on a railway bridge. Sams then pulled it down and rode off on a motorbike.

The two-way radio link failed and the coppers came in for a lot of stick about how he'd been allowed to get away. But from the time she'd been held the girl had learned a lot about Sams and the place where he worked and they got him in Newark about a month later. Turned out he had an artificial leg and he'd been thinking about doing a ransom for the better part of twenty years. He'd met Donald Neilson, the one they call the Black Panther, in prison and reckoned he was going to succeed where the other had failed.

In fact he was an all round failure because Julie Dart had fought back and he'd had to kill her because she'd recognised him. The week before that, apparently, he'd gone after another estate agent in Crewe and a builder who was working on the house more or less chased him off.

Whilst he was in the nick he'd taken a screw hostage, not that there's that much harm in that, and he got an eight on top of his lifes for that. Now here he is getting three thousand odd quid in a settlement from the Home Office saying that when he got moved between jails, paintings he'd done in the nick were lost. He must be a good artist if they'd fork that out. Apparently they were going to have a hearing in the nick where he was rather than take him out of Durham and to a local court. What with security and guarding the judge whilst he was in the nick it would have cost a packet and they can't have thought it was worth it.

It amazes me how he's got this settlement. If he's genuinely entitled to it then by all means let him have it, but he must be some painter and a half. Sounds like a bit more blackmail. It would cost more than it was worth to fight the case. It hurts me to say he should be paid. I'd kill him willingly. If he's got a fake leg then I'd do him over the head with it.

That's what I should have done when my stuff went missing at the end of my twenty-year sentence. I had a decent watch Hilly bought me, it was a cracker. I had a good fountain pen and all, cufflinks. Everything had disappeared. When I went to the gate that last morning they said I couldn't have them now; they couldn't find them. Later they said they'd looked in all the safes in the nicks where I'd been. It wasn't until 1970 or so that you could have your watch with you. I couldn't see the point. I always thought it was a headache looking at your watch, seeing how slow time was passing. And with all them thieves about I thought it would be safer in the Chief's safe. But I was wrong.

26 January 1962

I met Lucky Luciano twice in my life. Both times it was in Rome and both times I was with Albert Dimes and, more important, Bert Marsh, the man whose real name was Papa Pasquale and who, once Darby Sabini had more or less retired after he'd done that bird in Lewes during the war, was the real man behind the Italians in Soho.

I remember Luciano as being not much bigger than me. He'd got a mop of hair on him and he'd got very neat hands and feet. He came to New York in 1906 and joined up with Meyer Lansky and Bugsy Siegel. By the 1930s there wasn't no gambling enterprise, no dock racket, no garment district extortion racket conducted without Luciano's authority and cut.

He was a bit unlucky he got done on vice charges and they may not have been all that kosher. According to the Pros, Luciano took out young working-class girls, waitresses, manicurists, shop-girls, and gave them a good time before making them pay for their release from their drab existences. He also made them pay for the heroin to which he had introduced them, turning them over to his subordinates. Anyway he gets sent to Italy during the war.

In 1943 they let him out of the maximum security prison Dannemora to Great Meadows penitentiary to help in the preparation of the invasion of Sicily. He got a grand send off from New York. It was in grand style, with Frank Costello and Meyer Lansky on the dock to wave him off. After the war he was in and out of Havana organising things. It's said he was the one who agreed his old mate Bugsy Siegel should get done after he spent so much building that hotel in Las Vegas.

What he did, though, was he pulled one stroke too much. On 26 January 1962 Luciano died at Naples' Capodicino airport. He had gone there to meet the producer of a potential film of his life. The official reason for his death was a heart attack, but a lot of people think that his coffee may have been poisoned to stop him telling too much.

There've been one or two deaths over here which have been a bit suspect. There was that Charles Taylor who died whilst he was on trial at the Old Bailey on a fraud charge. Found dead on the Underground. He was a friend of Billy Hill's and I knew him quite well. A real crook with cards, him and Billy. They could make them stand to attention. There's a story that he took some Scottish businessman for every penny he had and then the deeds of his factory, gave him £100 and a ticket to Canada at the end, but I don't know if it's true. Charles was well in with crooked cops as well and he had a hotel in Streatham where they did their drinking.

29 January 2000

I see Mickey Duff's autobiography came out the other week. I knew him a bit and it reminded me of some villainy I did with an old boxing promoter some time ago. I knew this one through Jim Wicks, who was Henry Cooper's manager, and Bert Marsh.

When Mickey Duff started the Anglo-American he banned Ronnie and Reggie after the first show and they screamed that they were no worse than I was. I'd gone with Charlie and Eddie. To his credit Mickey said 'No' to banning me.

Sometime in 1962, just after I came out from the Spot thing, I and another put some gelignite and detonators at the ringside of a big tournament. We got in early and in them days there was no security – this was well before the IRA – and there was hardly anyone arrived. We put it under the chairs where the press was going to sit but we never joined them up. No one took the slightest notice of us. Out we came and I got in a call box and rang the police and said in a hard voice there was a bomb and that it was 'Because I don't like boxing'. Then I was well away before they could trace the call. After that there was no option but to search. Really it was to do a favour to a rival promoter. It didn't ruin the show but it caused the man a bit of grief.

Jelly was easy enough to come by then, mostly came from the mines in Scotland or sometimes Wales, and safes could still be blown with something tasty in them when you did. Now all you'd find is the account books. I think Alfie Fraser, who was no relation, was the best safeman I ever knew. One of the ones he did was St Martin's bank off Piccadilly. Eddie Chapman, who died the other year, who worked behind German lines during the war and who was with Billy Hill for years, was good but he wasn't up to Alf.

As for me I never had no luck with safes at all. There's some people who say Johnny Ramensky, the Scots geezer who was a great escaper, was the best and, of course, he trained Paddy Meehan who I knew from Arthur Thompson in Glasgow. Before the war Johnny was sent to Peterhead where the regime was every bit as bad as at the Moor. Warders carried sabres and if you got within five feet of one the man drew it. The regime wasn't much better in other prisons, and when some geezer from Glasgow tried to escape in 1932 the warder who shot him dead got off completely. He'd been doing his duty. It was only after a warder got shot by another, when he was aiming at a prisoner and the bullet ricocheted, that they banned the screws from having guns altogether. After Johnny's first escape in 1934 he was put in shackles for weeks. They locked them to the wall at night and he had to wear them when he had a bath. It was only after some MP took it up with the Home Secretary that they unchained him.

Johnny was another who had a good war record. In 1942 he was let out to join the army on secret missions. He had his name changed to Ramsey and he was dropped behind enemy lines to blow safes to get at top secret documents. When the Allies marched into Rome Johnny did fourteen safes and a strongroom in different buildings in the day. He also blew open the safes at Hermann Goering's headquarters in the Schorfhleide.

But his problem was he was a compulsive breaker. Even on his way home after his discharge from the army he didn't seem to be able to help himself. They demobbed him in York and gave him a travel warrant to go home to Glasgow but he never made it for years. He'd heard of a safe in York that was said to be burglarproof and it was too much of a challenge. He blew it all right but the police arrived whilst he was pulling the stuff out of it. He got five years and was only out five minutes – well it was actually seven days – before he got another five for blowing a post office near Glasgow. At least he'd got to see his family.

In 1955 he got another ten for a safe up in Oban and by this time he'd married. He couldn't believe the harshness and that first year he escaped three times from Peterhead. With his two previous escapes before the war this meant he'd actually got out five times. This last was just before Christmas and he managed to stay out till Boxing Day. Well, actually he wasn't out because he was lying under the floor of the prison doctor's office. Then when he thought it was safe he came out on Boxing Day and was over the wall. Just like people on Dartmoor don't like turning escapers in, Johnny reckoned he was so popular that they'd turn a blind eye at least coming up to New Year, but when he hitched a lift the lorry driver lollied him. The prison governor got into awful hot water over how Johnny'd got out of his nick so often, but I have to say he was a decent fellow. He argued that if you put Johnny in an open prison he wouldn't escape because there'd be no challenge, but the authorities weren't having none of it and Johnny did the remainder of his nine years in Peterhead. He was still doing safes when he was in his late sixties when he got twenty months. His brief said he'd been on more roofs than Topol. He died in Perth nick during the sentence.

4 February 2000

I went down to give a talk at the City of London University today. I've done it every year for the last three or four years. It's organised by Gary Mason the editor of *Police Review*, who lectures there of a Friday, and that's a funny thing because normally I wouldn't shake hands with anyone who's anything to do with the police. But I enjoy it. It's kids in the journalism school and they ask me questions and then have to do a write-up interview with me. Sometimes they'll contact me afterwards and do a longer follow-up. It's interesting the questions they ask. Today was about Dr Shipman, the GP who did all those patients. Gary said they might ask about Jill Dando, but in fact they didn't. What I said about Jill Dando to Gary was that if it was a contract, and I didn't believe it was, it wasn't a real professional one. I can't believe a professional would have taken the chances the man did. He'd have had a car, with bent plates, parked overnight in the road, aimed at an easy getaway. Still, since you can take out a contract at a grand these days, perhaps it wasn't a pro.

Gary met me at the Angel tube station and we passed the Empress of Russia on the way to the talk. The pub's being done up now but back in the 50s it was where the crooked screw from Pentonville did all his business. He was a lucky man for a lot of his time, and so far as prisoners was concerned he was a good one. He'd bring in snout for them. Johnny Isaacs, who was known as the Prisoners' Friend, was the middle man. He'd meet him in the Empress and do the business for the families. Poor old Johnny got done in Hoxton in 1965. He got shot over a bird. He'd been out drinking with Bobby Warren and someone done him on the way home. I think a man got charged but I can't be sure. As for the screw he led a charmed life for years. He got promoted and promoted and ended as a principal at Canterbury. Someone told me he eventually got done himself but I don't know. You hear all these stories.

I've lectured at schools and universities all over the country since the first book come out. Once, when I went up to Hull, there was a terrible scream because the local papers thought I was being paid £500. Of course I wasn't. I didn't even take any exes. People were saying what was the university doing having criminals like me talking to the students. The answer was quite simple. I was talking to the criminology class, and if you're studying something like that meeting a real live criminal, even a retired one, has to be better than just reading about it in the books. For a start they were a bit leery of me. I think they thought I was having them on about some of the exploits but when we got talking about self-mutilation in prison I rolled up my sleeves and showed them where you can still see eighty stitches in either arm, where I did myself all those years ago in Pentonville. After that they paid attention.

I'm always being asked why I should be making still more money out of crime. Personally I've no regrets. I give the public what it wants. People don't have to come and see my shows and they don't have to buy the books, but I'm glad to say they do. If they didn't I'd soon be on the dole or looking for a bit of work. Anyway look at it as a piece of social history.

6 February 1970

I was in Leicester with one of the Hosein brothers for a bit. He kept very much to himself. It was a brilliant idea that kidnap – but not in practice and the way they went about it. For a start they kidnapped the wrong woman.

There were two of them. Arthur, who was the smaller and the dominant one, you'll see what I mean about small men, and Nizam who was bigger and more stupid. He was the muscle. Originally the pair of them came from Trinidad with their father and Arthur had a farm, Stocking Pelham, out near Bishops Stortford in Hertfordshire, which is where they took Mrs McKay who they snatched in mistake for Rupert Murdoch's wife just before New Year 1970. That bit wasn't too bad, because her husband was a chief executive with Murdoch's papers and so there was still plenty of money to be had for the ransom, but it all went wrong.

They was complete amateurs and, when it came to it about kidnappings in them days, the police weren't that much better. They started sending ransom notes and the police tried to fool the Hoseins by giving them only a tiny bit of genuine money. The Hoseins smelled a rat and wouldn't go near it. Not surprising – they had policemen dressed as Hell's Angels riding up and down on bikes. Next time they demanded half a million. That drop went wrong again, though by all accounts it wasn't the police's fault. No one had told the locals and when they found the two suitcases full of money they rang the police and stood guard over it.

The Hoseins had a look and drove off but this time the coppers saw the numberplate and the brothers got nicked on 6 February. They was so stupid they was using their own car. The coppers reckon she was shot on New Year's Day and fed to the pigs. Funnily enough, there was another killing at that farm a few years later. Someone gatecrashed a wedding party and got done with a sickle.

You couldn't ever get much out of Hosein and, personally, I think they still thought that if there wasn't a body you couldn't be convicted. That was the way it used to be in case the Pros said you topped someone and they turned up later.

There was a case just after the Civil War like that. Some servant disappeared and three people got topped. One of them was meant to have confessed but I suppose they tortured it out of him. Then, whilst they were still swinging from the gibbet, the man they're supposed to have done turns up with a fanny that he'd been kidnapped by pirates and taken to Turkey and had to work in a harem or something rubbish like that.

From then on there was a no body, no crime rule and that lasted until after the last war. The courts had already decided that if the killing happened at sea there didn't need to be a body – like when that steward who'd been having it off with a passenger who'd died whilst they were at it pushed her through the porthole. But it was another farmer who was the one who had the rule changed.

He was a Pole, called Onjufreczyk, and after the war he set up in partnership with another Pole farming in Wales. They didn't get on and so he killed his partner who was wanting his money back. There was some blood in the kitchen but nothing much else and Onjufreczyk said the man had gone back to Poland.

They brought him up at Swansea Assizes and the jury accepted the circumstantial evidence, but the authorities can't have been that happy the man wasn't going to come walking back one day, or turning up behind the Iron Curtain, because they reprieved him. I never met him in the nick but I knew plenty of people who did. Ronnie Diamond, who was a great pal of the Nash family, he was one, used to say Onjufreczyk taught him chess and that he was a brilliant player.[1]

There were lots of disappearances when I was working and of course all sorts of rumours where the bodies got to. There was Jack 'The Hat'; of course, there must be more theories about that than I've had hot Christmas dinners as to where he's got to. Crushed into a cube in one of them car breakers yards, buried at sea, in a double grave somewhere. Then there's Ginger Marks. People say he's part of a flyover on the M4. He disappeared just outside the Repton Boxing Club where I take people on my tours. His was just bad luck, of course. He got shot when he was with Jimmy Evans, who'd earlier shot Freddie Foreman's brother, George,

---

[1] The old case Fraser refers to is the 1660 Camden Wonder when Joan, Richard and John Parry were convicted of the killing in Chipping Camden, Gloucestershire, of William Harrison. It is now thought that Harrison had stolen his employers' money and thought it prudent to disappear. In 1948 in what was known as The Port Hole murder case, James Camb, a steward on the *Durban Castle*, was convicted of killing a passenger, Gay Gibson. The prosecution's case was that there was a violent struggle during which Camb strangled the actress. Sentenced to death at a time Parliament was considering abolishing capital punishment, Camb was reprieved. In the 1961 case of Onjufreczyk the reason for the reprieve was indeed the fear that someone from behind the Iron Curtain might claim to be the supposedly deceased victim, Stanislaw Sykut. Onjufreczyk was released in 1965. He went to live in Bradford, where the next year he was killed in a car accident.

and Marks got shot by mistake. Mad Teddy Smith, who was a great mate of the Twins, was another who just disappeared. People say it was a quarrel over a boy.

But it's always possible that some of them will come back. Look at Jimmy Moody, who was with me on the night Dickie Hart got killed. Vanished out of Brixton prison and no one knew where he'd gone for years and years. Then it turns out he's been working in the community all the time, until he gets shot down the East End. He'd gone for the best part of twenty years.

Crematoriums were the favourite in Billy Hill's day. People would get in touch with him and he had one of the staff straightened up in a crematorium over in Putney, not far from where he lived, in fact. He'd get him to open up the furnaces a bit early and we'd give the man the soldier's farewell and scatter the ashes outside Wandsworth nick. No one was the wiser. Bill put a good number away. Maybe only two or three a year, but it adds up. I was in the nick a lot of the time and when I came out he didn't tell me everything and I didn't ask too closely, but he did name some names. I wouldn't want to say who they were because they'll still have loved ones, but they were all crooked or half-hooky anyway. But you couldn't do it that way now. The story leaked out over the years and there's too much security about for it to happen now.

7 February 1960

This was the day of the Pen Club shooting down in Duval Street, Spitalfields. Selwyn Cooney got shot dead and there was some very famous names involved. Billy Ambrose and Jerry Callaghan from Walworth had bought the club with the proceeds of a robbery at the Parker Pen Company, and it was a hangout for faces from both sides of the river. It's difficult to know the real reason behind it all, but it may have been a personal thing and it may have been a bit of a trial of strength after Billy Hill more or less called it a day. Cooney used to manage the New Cabinet Club in Gerrard Street for Aggie Hill, Bill's wife. He had a quarrel with Ronnie Nash from the big Clerkenwell family over who should pay a car bill, and a week or so later Cooney was shot down the club.

Fay Richardson was managing the place. She was a funny girl; nothing to look at at all but she had some sort of magnetism which pulls men in. The trouble with her was that most of them ended up in a bad way. I know she'd had convictions for brassing but she wasn't really a tom. There again she wasn't a hoister, certainly she wasn't top-class at that time. She was really a club girl. What we'd call a Monday groupie. Monday was the day when the markets all over London closed and the people who worked the stalls would be in clubs drinking along with the rest of us. Fay liked being along.

Back in 1956 she went and fell for Tommy Smithson who got cut so badly down Camden Town. She met him when she was a brass's maid and, so she said, she wasn't working herself. Then she went and got herself done over a load of cheques and, even though she'd got no form except for tomming, they locked her up in Holloway till the trial. Tommy Smithson, who used to mind the Maltese clubs down the East End for them, started a collection fund to pay for her defence. He'd got Bill Hemming to defend her. Hemming was an old copper who'd become a brief. I think he was the first ever to do so and he knew the ropes all right. But he didn't do work on legal aid and he charged steep enough. He was involved in the Challenor inquiry after my boy got into trouble. Tommy Smithson goes round the clubs with a book putting down who's made donations and how much. George Caruana, who became very big indeed, doesn't give enough and Tommy leaned on him a bit heavy. Had someone hold a gun on him and his minder Philip Ellul whilst he cut him. A bit under a fortnight later Tommy's shot dead in the gutter. They say his last words were 'Good morning, I'm dying'. Years afterwards Ellul got done for the murder and got reprieved. As for Caruana, the Twins tried to have him blown away at the Old Bailey where he was a witness and after that he pushed off to Germany and did a double act with his wife in some club there. He thought he'd be safer there and he was probably quite right. It wasn't nothing personal against Caruana. They were doing it as a favour for Bernie Silver, who was big in vice at the time.

Of course Tommy's death helped Fay no end and she got probation. Lots of tears and sadness. It was a big send off and she sent a wreath saying 'Until we meet again'. They hadn't let her go to Tommy's funeral and the papers made a big thing about how she was visiting his grave before she went back North where she come from.

Another of the men she went out with was Jack Rosa. He ended up getting killed in a car crash. Nothing to do with her, of course, but it shows what luck her men had. He was another with good dying words. He'd got a bent licence and when the copper comes to find him he says 'It wasn't me who was driving'. Game to the last, Jack. Once he'd been a great pal of mine. Eva put him up after he come out of Broadmoor, but that still didn't stop him doing her husband little Jimmy Brindle, in the Reform Club down the Elephant years later. Mind you he was gone by then. He'd been on the drink so long. Eddie and Charlie Richardson went round and really done him for that.

Then Fay came back down to London and married a geezer named Richardson who worked for some clubs in Paddington. That's when she went to work at the Pen Club. The night of the fight, Cooney's shot and so is Billy Ambrose, who was a very promising boxer before the Board took his licence off him after he did a bit of bird. That was the end of him and after that he got done for a couple of robberies. But Bill lived all right. He's taken to the London Hospital and Fay goes and puts herself right in it by going there and saying she's Mrs Patrick Callaghan. Then when she's questioned she puts Jimmy Nash, Ronnie's brother, the one they call Trunky because of his nose, in the frame.

Next thing is Fay goes into hiding. She doesn't turn up at the trial and Jimmy gets slung for the murder and five years for thumping Cooney. Billy Hill wanted to pay for Cooney's funeral but his dad wasn't having it.

Once it was over Fay surfaced all right and gave an interview about how she was giving up club life. In the end she went to Australia. She was finished over here. She'd gone hooky but even though she half tweedled it, she wasn't to be trusted no more. Someone told me she come over with an Australian mob a few years ago but if she did I never saw her. As for Billy Ambrose he went to the States and did very well over there for a time because he had some good connections, but I hear he's back now. Jerry Callaghan was a great mate of Alfie Gerard and they had it on their toes to Australia when they were wanted for bashing some coppers. Poor Jerry died a bit ago. He'd been in a wheelchair for some time. Alfie Gerard died years back in Brighton. Jimmy and the other Nash brothers are big in straight business now.

14 February 1984

Of course the most famous killing on St Valentine's Day was in 1928 when Capone had Bugsy Moran's mob, who was the opposition, wiped out in that garage which they used as an office in Chicago. But there's been some other really good killings on both sides of the Atlantic.

Over the previous months in Chicago there'd been terrible trouble between Capone and his mob and Bugsy Moran. Al got 'Machine Gun' Jack McGurn, Frank Scalesi and Al Anselmi and a couple of members of the Purple Gang from Detroit to see Moran and the others off. They went into a garage disguised as police officers, lined them up against a wall and blew them away. In fact Bugsy Moran survived because he was late for work – which is as good a recommendation for not turning up on time as I know. If I'd been there I'd have copped it because I don't think I've been late for a meet more than a couple of times in my life. No one ever got nicked for it. Capone had made sure he was down in Florida when it went off.

Not too many came out of it too good. Within three months Anselmi and Scalesi, along with a guy Joey they called Hop Toad, got beaten to death by Capone and Tony Accardo, who they called Batters afterwards, at a dinner which was supposed to be in their honour.

'Machine Gun' Jack got done in a bowling alley in 1936. Funnily enough it was the day after Valentine's Day but someone still left a comic card by his body. Bugsy lived on but he got caught for a bank robbery and died in the penitentiary in 1957.

It's never been quite clear which side of midnight the Montreal Valentine's Day Massacre of 1975 happened. The Dubois brothers were a family of nine brothers led by Claude, who ran protection and drugs in the city. They made the Twins look small. At any one time they could have two hundred men working for them and Claude would have them meet at 7 p.m. sharp on Thursdays, Fridays and Saturdays. The brothers were having trouble with Paul McSween, who'd worked with them for some time but had gone and set up his own team. That night the Dubois' men just turned up at the South Shore Hotel and opened fire. They took out four of the oppo. No one was ever nicked to my knowledge.

Over here David Elmore, who was a nightclub bouncer, and Jimmy 'The Wad' Waddington vanished in 1984. The Pros said it was all over a quarrel between the Elmores and a family called Maxwell – not the publisher – which had started ten years earlier when Mickey Maxwell had been done with an axe. It's not just the Italians who run these vendettas. Think how long the quarrel between the Brindles and the Carters lasted – what was it, the better part of fifteen years? Elmore was the target and The Wad just happened to be in the wrong place at the wrong time. They called him The Wad because he always had a wad of dough on him wherever he went. They had a right going over. They was bound hand and foot, given a cutting with a sword, and then strangled with a tablecloth. It all happened in the Kaleli, a Turkish restaurant in Station Road, Barking, which doesn't sound all that romantic. The Pros got a witness who said that Elmore was so scared he started reciting the Lord's Prayer and when he got to 'Thy will be done' one of the geezers who was doing them interrupted him and said 'You're dead right, son'. The Pros had a second theory in case the feud story didn't wear with the jury, and they were saying that Elmore was running a protection racket.

David Maxwell and David Reader, who was said to have helped dispose of the bodies, were nicked and got chucked at the Bailey. David said there was no proof either of the men was dead anyway. Not quite their bodies turned up, but both the heads did. Someone lobbed them at Harold Hill police station after the trial was over. Jim's mum was upset. She'd wanted her boy to be found in one piece and who could blame her?

15 February 2000

I was pleased to see Charlie Bronson got out of that attempted murder but I suppose it was inevitable he'd got done for kidnapping a screw. After all you can't lock them up in your cell and expect to get away with it. His real name was Mickey Peterson, not the same guy who was done in the Parkhurst trial with me. He changed his name by deed poll to be like the actor. This time he was done for a screw who he'd kidnapped and he'd kept in his cell. The screw had offended him by criticising an anti-AIDS poster he'd drawn. It was a bit like me at Parkhurst. If I'd gone down for incitement to murder or GBH with intent I don't think I'd ever have got out. They'd have lifed me off and that would have been the end. As it was I got another five years and there was a bit of light even though it meant a twenty in all.

Funnily Bronson wasn't that much of a face until they stuck him away. I only met him when I was doing bird for the coins after I come out from the twenty. He come up to me as if he knew me well. If I had bumped into him before I can't remember. He'd just got a seven. What he'd done as far as I can tell is he'd done a jewellers and then a fortnight later gone back and done it again. The girl told him they'd been to the police but he wouldn't have it. It was like knocking on the door of the nick and saying 'Let me in'.

My boy, Frank, was with him in Belmarsh when Bronson got done over the Arabs or Iraqis, whatever. That was a few years back. 1996 I think. He'd been allowed the run of a few cells and he was doing a bit of sweeping outside them when he said to his mate Jason Greasley to bring a couple of Iraqis who've been done for hi-jacking over to him and pushes them all in the cell, ties them up and then barricades himself in. Told the screws if they didn't meet his demands they'd need four body bags. Then when the negotiators turn up he says he wants to go to Cuba. After that he wants a helicopter to go to Heathrow and a jet to Libya. Eventually he released them all but he still drew another seven.

It's sad because before this he was due out in 2005 which he could see. Now he's working up never to be let out. But, there again, does he want to be?

7 March 1966

I'll never understand what got into Dickie Hart that night in Mr Smith's Club over in Clapton. The night before, Eddie Richardson and I had just agreed to look after the club for that Manchester businessman, Owen Ratcliffe, and his partner. We were going to be allowed to put some of our machines in the club and later, when it was making a profit, take a cut. In the meantime we had to make sure there was no trouble. In the early hours Dickie just started shooting during a perfectly ordinary straightener between Eddie and Peter Hennessey, one of the brothers. He and Eddie Gardner had sent out for guns. People have said Dickie was a Kray man but you can take that with a great pinch of salt. He was a good thief, that's certain. You couldn't fault him. Good-looking, a bit under six foot and he had a good name. I knew him when he came to the Bonsoir, a club I had for a time with Gilbert France and Albert Dimes in Gerrard Street, just below where you go into Shaftesbury Avenue. I remember one night he ran up a bill, hadn't got enough money on him and we just gave him tick. We knew he was good for it and, sure enough, two days later he came in and paid up.

Then that night he just runs out and gets a gun and starts blazing away in something which wasn't anything to do with him at all. Then he shoots me in the thigh. Of course, he'd been drinking but even so. There was no alternative for me but to shoot him myself and it was right I was acquitted. After that it was all hands to the pump. Some ran out the front door and some out the back and I limped as best I could with me leg half off down the road, which was full of little terraced houses. The coppers got themselves in a right mess over the evidence. One copper says he saw me in the garden with the gun next to me and another copper says the first one wasn't there at all. When it come to it I'd thrown the gun away in a garden about fifty yards from where I was found.

Quite a lot of us got away at first, but Jimmy Moody and Billy Stayton – who were trying to help me – they stayed behind. Luckily they got chucked. Ronnie Jeffrey wasn't so lucky. He got shot but at least he got a not guilty at the end of it all. Of course Dickie Hart didn't move. Eddie, who'd been shot in the leg, got taken to hospital and that's where he got nicked. So was Harry Rawlings, who was in a bad way. He'd been shot as well but he got out of it too.

I suppose, in a way, I came out best because I was in such a bad way, because for a time they couldn't question me, couldn't verbal me up. By the time they did their boat had gone. They'd missed it.

Jimmy Fellowes, my brief, was brilliant. At first there was a local superintendent in charge of the case, but then who shows up at my bedside but Tommy Butler – who'd done the Train Robbery investigation. When he came to interview me in the hospital wing Fellowes made me put earphones on so I couldn't hear the questions. It didn't half annoy Butler. You couldn't get away with that now. They'd probably try to do us both for conspiracy to pervert the course of justice.

After Dickie died his widow married Stan Naylor, who went down with the Tibbs over their quarrel with the

Nicholls. Stan was with me when I was at Chelmsford and we'd be in the same visiting room when she came on a visit. But she was a good woman, never made any difficulty. Really I think people regarded Dickie as just a bit unlucky and there wasn't really no blame attached to me. Last I heard, Stan had got involved with the French brothers from South London and after that he bought a farm.

All in all there's a few of us gone from that night. Peter Hennessey got stabbed to death at a boxing tournament in the Royal Garden Hotel in Kensington. There was sixty stab wounds by the time they took him to the mortuary. I wasn't there but most of the rest of South London was, and one account is that he was going round making a nuisance of himself, blagging people off collecting for another charity than the one the tournament was meant to be helping. He got into a quarrel with Paddy O'Nione and him and Jimmy Coleman from another big family, who was a brother-in-law of the Arifs, got done for the murder, but they were acquitted. Peter came from a good family. He and his brother Bernard had bought the Dog and Bell in Deptford and at Christmas they used to round up all the old dears who drank in the pub over the year – and a good many who didn't – and put them in a coach and take them to C & As in Lewisham and buy them a new hat and coat and a lunch. But Peter had a wicked temper and there was a lot of people frightened of him, including some of the local Old Bill.

Paddy O'Nione, who was known as Paddy Onions, didn't last that long after he was chucked. He went down in November 1982, shot near his son's wine bar in Tower Bridge Road. There was talk that Jimmy Davey did it, but he died in a choke hold in a police station in Coventry as he was waiting to be handed over to the London coppers to bring him back for questioning. The story the coppers put about was that Davey had done Onions for £5,000. We'll never know now.

I heard just recently from Charlie Richardson that Eddie Gardner who was there that night has died. He'd had cancer. I was well pleased. I don't mean exactly that I wanted him dead, but now he is I can't say I'm sorry. He was a big burly type of guy and he got a lot of us nicked when he didn't need to. He was one of the two who had guns that night, but his got taken away from him and he got done. That's no excuse for grassing, though. After all, Billy Hayward didn't put us in it and he could have done. Like I've said, he managed to get to Freddie Foreman and had his head sewn up. Once one of these things happens the decent people don't go running to the law. It's nothing to do with them. When it happens it may be you against another, but when you're nicked it's both of you against the law. The thing to do is get as many of you out as you can, not put them in it and that's what Gardner forgot.

Then there was Henry Botton who borrowed a pony off me just before the shooting started and then went and put me in the frame, giving evidence against me at the Bailey. He got five years for the fighting that night. He got both barrels one night in July 1983 at his home in Shooter's Hill, Deptford, and I can't say I was sorry at all. It was just as well I was in the nick because I'd have had the blame if I'd been out. I was in the chokey in Durham when I heard the news and it made my bit of bread taste better that night. As I heard it, he'd given evidence at someone else's trial and the man's friends had the hump. But there was another story, that he pulled a stroke over some bit of villainy and the other people took umbrage. Billy Clarkson was the organiser and he got twenty-five years minimum. He'd got a kid to dress up as a copper and when Henry went to the door – bang.

Jimmy Moody, who tried to get us away from the scene and who got a not guilty, is dead as well. Shot in June 1994 over in East London by a man who just came in the bar and did him. I knew it was on Jim but there was nothing I could do if I wanted to. I just packed my bags and went North for a couple of days. I hadn't seen him in years. I'd had a card from him after he escaped from Brixton with the IRA guy and Stan Thompson, who was on the Parkhurst Trial with me, but I hadn't seen him. When it came to it, the shooting was a personal thing. He'd done someone badly and it was a reprisal. It must be one of the few killings of its kind that the police never came to talk to me about.

Eddie Richardson got done on a very big cannabis smuggling and he won't be out until 2006 at the earliest. He was always artistic and he's got better over the years and has won quite a few prizes for the paintings he's done.

Billy Stayton just disappeared. I don't mean that in the bad sense, but he just drifted away. Billy Hayward, who the police say was protecting the place before Eddie and me took over that night, is still around. I see him quite often. His brother Harry still has the Harp of Erin. He rang me the other day about the film about my life. He said he'd heard it was definite and would I leave him out since his wife was still giving him murders about that night. Roy Porritt, who was with us and who unbeknowingly started it all, I think, because the Haywards thought he'd got the hump with Billy, he's dead. Natural causes. Harry Rawlings, the one who Hart shot first, is still about as well. If you'd seen him that night pumping blood you wouldn't have thought he could have made it.

8 March 1966

The day after I was nicked over Dickie Hart's murder, the first thing I had to do was get a message out. Getting the info out was difficult because if you were on a murder charge you had your visits in the prison hospital visitors' room at a big table about twenty feet long with you at one end, your visitor at the other and the screws hearing every word you said in the middle of you. And they took notes. They had to keep a book about anyone in for murder. What they did, when and why.

So the first problem was getting the message out and the only safe way to do it was through a brief and that's what I did with Jimmy Fellowes, from Walthamstow. He acted for me over the years; helped me out when I was on the run from that bit of trouble in Brighton, when I'd burned down a bingo hall in Eastbourne for Harry Rogers and then he wouldn't pay me. Said I was demanding money with menaces. Jimmy Fellowes sorted all that out for me. He got me a not guilty and my costs without it ever going to trial.

What he also used to do was let me sleep in his office if I come to see him of an evening. I never liked driving and I was down in the Brighton area most of the time, so I'd sleep all night in one of the chairs in his waiting room and then let meself out in the morning before the staff arrived.

Anyway, this was more serious. I didn't want to put Jimmy in it and so I said something like 'You might tell Eva to get rid of that old heavy luggage. It don't look like I'll be needing it for a bit and there's no point in having it around'. She'd get the message and know what to do and, if anything did go wrong, then Jimmy wouldn't be compromised. He could say quite genuinely he thought it was a suitcase or whatever. Of course he wasn't that daft. He'd know full well there was something in it but it gave him an out. There was briefs you could do that with and there was briefs you couldn't, and Jim was one of those you could. That's why the coppers wouldn't let you see a brief for days on end if they could help it. The other reason was so they could verbal you up. All this was before that Act when they said you had to have a brief if you were going to be questioned. Look at that Terry Dewsnap who got shot. Very good thief he was, related somehow to Joe Wilkins. When he was wanted for a bank raid in Luton they had him moved all over the country so his brief couldn't find him until they were ready.

Why did I need to get a message out? Because I'd got a store of guns, hand grenades and flame throwers. I didn't have them in my place, of course. They was well distanced but it wasn't fair to the people who was doing the minding and who might get a spin just because they knew me. They all went in the Union Canal in Camberwell. God knows what went in there over the years. Safes, guns, ammo, the lot. It's like I said, we had enough ammo to start a small war and if we'd known there was going to be trouble at Mr Smith's we'd have gone in with weapons.

It wasn't that easy to get a gun. There's guns and guns, however. It depended on what sort you wanted. Of course, shotguns were no trouble. After all they were more or less legal and you could do a bit of work on them yourselves.

As for a revolver, that was more difficult. The trouble was you had to be very careful where you got them and who you got them off. The man might not be able to keep his box of tricks shut one hundred per cent. Then there was no telling who'd used them first and I've always liked a clean knife and fork. If you weren't going to use it yourself, only wave it about, well that might not be too bad unless you were caught with it. Then the police might start checking up to see if it had been fired before. The price would depend on how quick you wanted it. It was always best not to buy but get it from someone you trusted, and on condition that if when it came to it you didn't use it you'd return it, and if you had to then you'd get rid of it and pay him. You could get a good clean gun in 24 hours.

Guns are always handy to have. There was an occasion when something happened and we didn't have guns. I don't think it had happened to me since I got caught out in the quarrels with the Carters in the late 40s. I got caught short without a gun and it had been a lesson to me. The other thing they got rid of, after Dickie Hart bought it, was a flame thrower. That was a useful thing to have. Produce that and it was such a shock you maybe didn't have to hurt people. It could cost a bomb but people was always coming round the office of me and Eddie Richardson's Atlantic Machines, the one-arm bandit business we had off the Tottenham Court Road. Some people was bringing in dead straight propositions but a good number weren't. I bought the flame thrower out of me own pocket. I was the eldest and I had the most experience and I thought it might come in handy and it did. It cost me a few bob.

Nine times out of ten, people who wanted machines came to us. If you was starting up a club then you'd probably get advice from someone say in the next town and, like as not, he'd have some of Eddie's and my machines in his club. The thing about the machines was they worked. A machine on the blink is not only making no money, it's causing problems with the punters. They don't want to see a sign: SORRY THIS IS OUT OF ORDER when all they're wanting to do is empty their pockets of small change with their mates and, with luck, cash a few notes as well.

Sometimes, of course, they had trouble with local bullies who just wanted to chance their arm and cause trouble, or wanted to have their own machines in the club. That was when the thrower came in handy. I think I only actually used it on two occasions. It was up North and we were having a bit of trouble with some people from Liverpool. We needed a snappy settlement and it got their attention straight away. I set them on fire, of course. They run away screaming and rolling on the ground trying to put one another out.

That's what you wanted. It showed you were determined. I used it a second time, but after that the word must have got around. In a way it was a good thing, because with it you only had to show it and you didn't have to hurt people.

Of course the arrest of Leslie McCarthy for trying to bribe a juror really meant the end of Altlantic Machines. With Leslie locked up along with the rest of us, there was really no one to run it. Eddie and me had been looking after Charlie Chester's Casino in Archer Street with Jackie Hayes, the son of old Timmy, on the door. Not long after we was nicked the Kray Twins grass, Albert Donoghue, went and cut him and there was a general outcry. Of course Charlie Chester was only a front for John James, whose club we also looked after up in Southport, but Charlie went to the press saying how he wasn't going to submit to any threats from gangsters. If it was intended as a take over nothing came of it. If the Twins had wanted it there was no one to stop them having it – Charlie certainly wouldn't and I don't suppose John James could – or possibly even the place in Southport.

9 March 1965

This was the day it all started to go wrong for the Twins, even though it didn't unravel completely until four years later. This was the day that Ronnie went and shot Georgie Cornell in the Blind Beggar. And there was no need. If they really was plotting against us then the Twins already had their way. Me and Eddie were locked up and so was Jimmy Moody and Charlie was out of the country. Georgie Cornell was a great man but he wasn't a leader. He'd have done nothing unless he was told to do it, and so far as we were concerned we'd got enough on our plates without worrying about Ronnie and Reggie.

Georgie came from the Twins' side of the water. He'd belonged more or less to the Watney Streeters but then he'd married Olive, a girl from South London, and had hooked up with us. He'd gone over the water to see Jimmy Andrews who'd been shot in the leg. Some people said Ronnie'd done that as well, but I think it was more a bit of domestic trouble.

Jimmy was a good fellow, come out of Clerkenwell. He was smaller than me even but he was a terror. The boxer Roy Shaw says in his book that the three to fear was me, Jimmy Essex and Jimmy Andrews. He did a seven over a post office in 1958 and when he come out

I was on the run over a bit of trouble I was having in Brighton, and so I sent my boy Frank down to the Moor to bring him back. He worked with Eddie and me on the machines. He'd got cancer but he didn't know it then. His thin and thick was starting to turn blue and he was always making jokes about it. He was dead within the twelve months. Frankie Shay, Reggie's brother-in-law, later married Jimmy's wife. His daughter married Tony Adams, the Arsenal player.

After George had been to see Jimmy he called in the Beggar and the rest is history.

It's funny how villains tend to be small and how the public think they're very big men. Of course there's exceptions – George and Alan Dixon were giants and Lennie McLean was a big man – but overall I can't think of many more really big men. I don't go five foot six and Jimmy Essex was small, with Billy Blythe even smaller and so was Jimmy Andrews. Roy Shaw, the fighter who went in with Lennie, and who was in the nick with me, isn't big and neither really is Freddie Foreman; a good bit of beef about him but he's not tall. The Twins were only middleweights. Ruby Sparkes wasn't big, nor for that matter was George Cornell, and given how ferocious he was Alfie Gerard wasn't a big man. Jimmy Tibbs was tall, but I think he was only a lightweight when he was in the ring. Eddie Raimo was another man who was smaller than me. He couldn't half have a ruck. He was with the Sabinis and then with the Whites. He put a glass in Billy Hill's face once and Bill had to have surgery. When Eddie was at his peak he was a man to be looked up to. Then in turn Jack Spot did him at Yarmouth races in 1946 when the battle with the Whites was beginning and after that Eddie just faded away.

Willie Malone was a big man, a big man in every way. He ran some of the docks and he had a straight business as well. He was very friendly with the Twins and he was a very good friend of Alfie Allpress. Willie offered up some good jobs. There was no real security on the gates of the docks, no TV cameras, back after the war. Half the place was hooky. That's where your father would want you to go. Either the docks or the print. That was good money. Sign on, creep out and have a booze up and creep back in to clock out. Eddie Shah put a stop to that. And after him Murdoch.

I did a robbery in the print once. The printers weren't ones who'd have a go. There'd be some friends of yours in the crowd holding them back saying, 'Don't be silly, Harry. Could be dangerous' and they'd swallow it.

Alfie Allpress, he was the cream, a real trier. He got fifteen years back in '62 or '63. He had the keys of a watchman at a bank near the New Kent Road and it all went on top somehow. He got some disease whilst he was in the nick and they let him out to die. He come from the East End, him and his brother Danny. I can't think which had Danny Jr. He was a good wheelman, tiny as well. He got put away by the grass Bertie Smalls and Danny had been Smalls' best mate. He got cancer shortly after he was home. I think when he died he was on bail for taking a mechanical digger to a cash machine in the walls of a few banks. Game to the end.

One man who was surprisingly big for his job and that was the cat burglar Peter Scott, the one who did Sophia Loren's jewels either alone or with Taffy Jones – depending on whose version you believe. He was a good climber for such a big man; had a lot of strength in his arms. Peter's out again now. He had a bit of trouble a few years ago when he got nicked with Russell, John McVicar's son, over a painting Russell had out of a West End art dealers and Peter tried to sell it back to the insurance company. Peter was a good sportsman; when he was out of the nick he was a tennis professional.

10 March 1965

Of course there was always a chance I'd be topped. It was unlikely. First, I'd got to be found guilty and then it was going to be a bit difficult seeing that I'd been certified as mad twice. Not that it had done Straffen any good. He'd been insane when he escaped from Broadmoor, but sane when he killed the little girl after he got out, so there was no guarantees.

There are only two kinds of murder and that's a fact. There's no three or four or one kind. If anyone can contradict me they're entitled to win the lottery. The first kind is the spur of the minute and the other sort is premeditated. The first sort doesn't think about the consequences and the second doesn't think he'll be caught because he's worked it all out.

During my time I've met a number of people who've been on trial for murder in the days when you could swing, and there's no one thought they was going to be topped. There's plenty of people come up to me when I've been in the prison hospital and said 'Do you think I'm going to be hung, Frank?' and I've answered 'Yes, if you get a guilty then there's a good chance'. I don't see any point in telling them anything but the truth. It doesn't do to gee them up so's they feel all the worse about it afterwards when it's all gone wrong for them. Better they faced up to it.

After they got a guilty and got back to the prison they were looked over by the prison doctor and then put into special clothing with no tie in case they tried to strangle themselves and no shoes with laces for the same reason. They got a pair of slippers. There weren't even any buttons on the jackets in case you tried to swallow them. There'd be two warders on duty all the time with the prisoner and they'd be there to play chess and draughts with them. There used only to be one until a condemned man tried to kill the screw who was with him and they didn't take any chances after that.[1]

They got a larger cell, of course, because the screws had to be in there with them. Usually it was two or even three knocked together, and they had their own lavatory. The man had to sleep with his hands outside the bed so he didn't do himself any damage. It was also meant to stop him giving himself a J Arthur, but the men I've known who got reprieved have told me the screws didn't seem to mind if they did. There wasn't much they could do to stop him, was there? No point in putting him down the punishment block, was there?

Almost everybody appealed, of course, and they made sure they was heard as quick as possible. They liked having a day out in the Strand so they could hear the appeal. There had to be at least three clear Sundays between the judge sentencing the person and the topping and once the appeal was down, unless you got to the House of Lords, which was very unlikely, all there was left was an application to the Home Secretary for a reprieve.

Then it was just a case of waiting and playing games with the warders. You could see the prison chaplain, of

---

[1] In 1890 Felix Spicer, who had been convicted of the murder of his two youngest children, tried to kill his guard and then himself in Knutsford gaol. The guard managed to give the alert and from that time there were always two guards in the condemned cell. Spicer was hanged by James Berry on 22 August at the same prison.

course, and doctors came and saw you and so did the prison governor but it was a case of 'Everything all right, man?' and nothing more. You got newspapers but they made sure you couldn't read any bit about your case.

After they were convicted you never spoke to them but I'd see them on exercise sometimes and I was surprised how happy they often looked. Really jolly – even one woman in Durham who'd poisoned a couple of her husbands. It was a famous case. I saw her out with the wardresses and she didn't look to have a care. Apparently they usually put on weight before they were topped.[2]

The question of a reprieve always took time and this was where your briefs could help, and sometimes a public petition would go in for you, but it didn't do much good as a regular thing. There was one where something like 80,000 people signed it but he still got topped. They liked to get things done as quickly as possible, but I was in the nick in Wandsworth in 1943 with that Canadian soldier who shot his girlfriend and he was in the condemned cell sixty days – which was the longest there ever was.

Wandsworth was strange. If for some reason they were coming out of the condemned cell, say to have a visit, they had to come for a few moments into the

---

[2] Married in 1914, Mary Knowles poisoned her first husband John in 1955. She then poisoned John Russell her lover-lodger in January 1956. A new husband, Oliver Leonard, a retired estate agent, followed in October that year. She poisoned the last, Ernest Wilson, in November the next year. She was convicted at Leeds Assizes in March 1958 but was reprieved by the Home Secretary. She was then aged 66 and it is possible her age assisted her. It may also have been Lord Butler's squeamishness over the wearing of rubber knickers by women on the scaffold. She was transferred to Holloway Prison where she died in 1962. See Richard Whittington-Egan 'The Widow of Windy Nook' in Jonathan Goodman (ed) The Lady Killers and Fenton Bresler, Reprieve.

prison proper and there would be a call 'All cleaners away'. That meant everybody, because in those days cell doors were always left open when people went to work. So you were just locked in the nearest cell until they had passed.

The condemned people had visits in Wandsworth in a double cell. They'd just walk a few steps whilst the visitors came through the gates, turned left and up on to E wing. There was no contact. It was all done through glass.

There was a clock at Wandsworth like most other prisons and it always struck on the hour. When I was on punishment on E4, when it struck ten o'clock at night that was when my friends lowered a bit of bread and cheese down to me. There were no outside night patrols in them days so they could only be caught if someone came in their cells. Once the orderly officer double-locked the prison no one came out until he took the double off the next morning.

On the night before an execution they stopped the clock at either ten or midnight and it never struck again until after he was executed. For them six weeks or whatever he would have heard the hours striking and then he'd never hear it strike again. I always thought that was cruel, but there again it may have been kind, so he never knew he'd got an hour less to live or how many there were to go. If anyone got a reprieve, as a general rule they would go into the prison hospital for a couple of weeks for assessment, and then go into the prison proper as a normal prisoner.

In 1948 I was in with Haigh, the acid bath murderer, before he got convicted. I'd been nicked over a torch and because I'd been certified insane and put in Cane Hill for a time they popped me in the prison hospital for my remand. It seems silly now that you could be kept in custody over a torch, let alone get six months for it. Once people on remand knew I'd been in a mental hospital and they could see there was nothing wrong with me and I didn't think I was Napoleon, they were all after me wanting to know how I'd done it. Working the trick of being certified, is what they wanted to know. That would stop them getting topped.

There was no counselling in those days. Ordinary people who were waiting trial for murder just couldn't stop talking about it. It was 'What do you think, Frank, this?' and 'What do you think Frank, that?' It wasn't just me they was asking either. It was anyone who happened to be around. They were preoccupied with it and I can't say I blame them.

Haigh had done a four for fraud before he got nicked for murder. He'd also done at least five people and possibly more. It was his own fault he got nicked for them. He was one of them who couldn't believe they'd get caught.[3] What he did was make up to a wealthy widow who lived in the same hotel in Earls Court and persuaded her to invest in a scheme for marketing false fingernails. He got her to go down for a drive to see his workshop in Crawley, and there he shot her and tipped the body in a drum of sulphuric acid. He thought that would melt her away. He also hadn't been reading the law books, because he thought if there was no body there could be no murder trial. He was wrong on both counts. Bad luck for him, the acid hadn't got rid of her completely.

The police took a dislike to him when they started interviewing the hotel residents and once they'd found the gun at his workshop it was all over for him. He tried to make out he was insane, saying in a statement that he liked drinking the victim's blood, but it didn't do him no good. He'd already knocked off five others and dumped them in the acid. He did it all for the money.

---

[3] John George Haigh was hanged at Wandsworth on 10 August 1949. Neville Heath was convicted of the murder of Margery Gardener and hanged at Pentonville on 26 October 1946.

I must say I'd never've thought Haigh would have been capable of the villainy he got up to. He was one who never talked about it. On the other hand I was also in with that RAF officer, Neville Heath, who liked whipping women and biting their nipples off. He was a cold fish. You would think he could do something like that. He was another who'd done a bit of time for fraud. The first one he did was a slapper in another Earls Court hotel. He'd beaten her with a whip and then mutilated her. In fact she died from suffocation. He pushed off to the South Coast and did a young girl he met in another hotel in Bournemouth. He was another who didn't think he could ever be convicted. One thing you have to say about Heath is he had style. When he's on the way to be topped he's offered a drink of whisky to help him see it through. 'Make it a double,' he says. That's why murder is such an extremely funny thing.

11 March 1991

When they got acquitted of murdering Turkish Abbi, the papers said I was the uncle of Tony and Patrick Brindle and, even though it's not true, they still say I am. There's dozens of Brindles all over South London. If I was related to those boys it could only be through Eva, and to my knowledge they're no relation of her husband. I suppose we could be third cousins once removed but that's about it. At the time their mother was pretty cross that they should be linked to an old villain like me, but when it comes to it they've had a fair number of troubles of their own.

The first of them was with that Turkish Abbi, whose real name was Ahmet Abdullah. The coppers said he was a drug dealer and the sort of informally adopted son of the Arifs. Abbi'd got up the nose of some other South East London family and he was shot in the William Hill betting shop in Bagshot Street, Walworth, on 11 March 1991 – not far from where I live now. He was hit in the back and he then tried to use another customer as a shield before he managed to escape from the shop. But once outside he was shot again. Tony and Patrick Brindle got nicked and at their trial at the Old Bailey witnesses gave evidence from behind screens and were only identified by numbers.

Tony said he'd never been in the betting shop that afternoon and he'd been playing cards in the Bell in East Street, Walworth, and Patrick didn't give evidence. Both of them got chucked but meantime a third brother, David, had been shot and killed whilst drinking in the Bell. My old friend Jimmy Moody, who helped me after Dickie Hart shot me, almost certainly did him. David had taken a bat to him a bit earlier, when he was working as a barman, and Jimmy had taken it off him and done him over. Now he was making sure there weren't any reprisals. And two years later Jimmy himself got shot in a pub down the East End. I knew it was on top but there was nothing I could do even if I wanted.

Life did not go well for that bit of the Brindles over the next few years. In 1995 Tony was ambushed and shot in Rotherhithe, where he had a flat, but this time police was on hand and they nicked a couple of people. Another brother, George, had survived being shot from a passing van earlier in the year. No one got nicked that time. When Tony was shot the coppers said it was a longstanding feud with the Dalys, who'd gone to Ireland. I'd known the Dalys, or at least their parents, for years. They came from round Waterloo. The Pros' case was that Peter Daly was living in Spain and he couldn't get any sense out of Tony Brindle so he sent over an ex-IRA man, Michael Boyle, to do him. There was even a story in *The Times* that I'd been hit during the quarrels, but if I was I felt no pain. Boyle picked up life at the Bailey in March 1997.

The last I heard David Brindle was trying to sue the police for damages for not getting to the gunmen sooner and he's got legal aid to help him do it. He's claiming the coppers should have told him he was at risk, but they said if they had done, he might have gone into hiding and when he came out things would be just as bad. Maybe they should have had me in their corner all along.

13 March 1984

David Martin was a funny man. He was really a loner but he became one of those 'most wanted men'. I knew him when he was in Wandsworth with me, and he wasn't really one of the boys at all. We all thought he was a right mug. He was just a hanger-on who wanted to be one of the chaps. That's what it seemed to be and then all of a sudden, bosch, he's up there in the headlines! Before that he was a joker. He'd snatch umarked police cars from right outside the nick, take them over to France and then give the station a bell and tell them where they could pick up their lost motor. Mind you, he done quite a bit of good work. He'd done time for some cheque frauds, done a Borstal for thumping a copper, and he'd tried to get out of Brixton using a dustbin as a battering ram. So, all in all, I suppose he had some credentials.

Then in August 1982 he was posing as a security man using the name of David Demain when he was fronted by a copper, and when he was told to empty his pockets he shot him point-blank in the cobblers. That's not a sensible thing to do. Shows he wasn't really a top pro. He was traced to Crawford Place in Marylebone where the police saw a woman in the entrance to a block of flats. In fact it was David in drag, and this time he opened fire with a semi-automatic and then with a Smith & Wesson. The coppers fired back and hit him in the head. They can't have injured him too bad, because whilst he was waiting trial he managed to get a duplicate key and get out of Marlborough Street magistrates' court in the West End near the London Palladium, when he was taken there for a remand hearing. Now, of course, he was really big. Sort of grew up overnight.

Then the police nicked him in a yellow Mini in Earls Court on 14 January 1983 after a tip off. They shot him five times and he got a pistol-whipping as well as he tried to get out of the Mini and away. That's what they thought anyway. The trouble was it wasn't David they'd shot. It was Stephen Waldeck, a film technician who they thought was Martin. And, worse for them, there was this solicitor in a car right behind who saw it all. David Sarch his name was, well overweight, red-bearded Irishman, who did a bit for me from time to time over the years; had a heart attack and died recently. Waldeck got quite a bit of loot in compensation and it wasn't for another fortnight that they found David.

Now the police had been tapping the phones of his friends and they discovered that he'd have his dinner in a place called the Milk Churn in Hampstead. David had really good senses and he thought there was something hooky, so he dived into the Underground, got on the line and headed for Belsize Park. Of course they switched the electricity off and went down after him. They found him in an alcove by the line. Funny thing, when they searched him all he had with him was a little penknife stuck to the roof of his mouth with chewing gum. He got 25 at the Old Bailey. He must have known he was in for a long stretch but he can't have thought it was going to be that long. He couldn't handle it and he topped himself in his cell on this day in 1984.

There's always stories about robbers who go around in drag and Martin was small enough to look like a woman. There was a team in Florida, the Ashley-Mobley gang, who did a series of banks around Orlando. They'd send in one of them disguised as a woman to start the hold up, but they're not all that common. I think it's the shame you'd have to endure if you got caught. There was a rumour that David was a pouf and that may have come from his dressing up as a girl. I remember there was an Irish team up Paddington way some years ago, pavement artists who were said to have someone in drag with them, but I think more likely it was one of their sisters – wild girl, she was.

19 March 1953

Billy Hill's wife Aggie was a nice woman. I always got on well with her She wasn't really good-looking but she had a lot of personality and, combined with what looks she had, that was enough to see her through. She put up with a lot from Bill and the marriage lasted over twenty years. Of course he had bits on the side but she coped with that and then he went and fell for Gyp.

As for her, Gypsy Riley, she was a cracker, really good-looking and real fire. There's a book which says that she was protected by an old Maltese known as Tulip before she took up with Billy Hill and that's possible.[1] If it's true it was before I knew her. The story is that Tulip approached her in a club and she had Slip Sullivan, one of the brothers from the East End, throw him out. The ponce got Tommy Smithson with him and, whatever you said about Tommy and how he was a loser who couldn't hold on to money, you could never say he wasn't dead game. There's also no doubt the Maltese used him as a minder so the story may have some foundation. He did Slip and now Gyp's temper was really up. She got hold of Billy to avenge Slip and in turn he got hold of Spotty. This was when they was talking to each other.

---

[1] Robert Murphy, *Smash and Grab* (1993) Faber and Faber, London.

They met Smithson round the back of the Craven A factory in Mornington Crescent, which was about home ground for Billy. Reports say there was Spot, Hilly, Dave Barry, the club owner from Paddington who did me such a good turn when the Carters put me in the frame, and a couple of Spot's mates like Moisha Blueboy. Some people say he was called Blueball because he had one but I never saw it and in fact I never heard him called that. They made Smithson give over his gun and when he'd done it Hill cut him really bad. He was spewing blood all over the place and for a time they thought they'd got a body on their hands. Spot give Smithson £1,000 to open another club and keep him quiet, but Tommy couldn't make a go of it. Next thing Smithson's cut a Maltese trying to make him pony up more money for the defence of Fay Sadler, the half brass he was with, and he gets shot for his pains. He didn't have a very lucky life.

By this time Aggie's on the way out. She and Hilly split and Gypsy took over. Hilly had also split with Spot and the fight had taken place in Frith Street. Then when Spot was trying to open in Paddington Gyp went and did a guy in the eye in the Miramar Club there. She got a not guilty from the magistrate today in 1953.

It may seem strange that I didn't know who ran which brass but they weren't really part of our world. By today's standards in those days the West End was empty; crowded by normal standards but empty. You'd see brasses in the clubs like Aggie's New Cabinet, but they weren't working. They were just having a drink same as everyone else and then they'd be back out to work. They had their bit of pavement, their pitch and they kept to it and woe betide any newcomer who tried to muscle in. Some of them girls couldn't half have a ruck. But it wasn't our game. If they had a ponce, and most of them was under the control of the Messina family, it was nothing to do with us.

21 March 1980

One thing that's never really happened over here has been the killing of the top men in power struggles. I know Jack Spot got cut up badly after he'd had a row with Albert Dimes but there was no real question of killing him. Billy Hill made sure I only had a shillelagh and not a knife that night. Most of the killings have been over domestics or women or insults. But in America they did each other night after night for business.

Angelo Bruno was one who got done. He'd run Philadelphia for years and had kept things quiet. Once, when someone tried to take him out and failed, he didn't even go after the man. He just made sure he was sent out of the city. I met Angelo a few times when he was over here, starting to run the gaming junkets. I was with Albert and I was like the man who stands behind the Godfather when the Dons meet after Sonny's been killed in the film and lights his cigar. It was all show. He was a great friend of Albert's and it was through him that Eddie Richardson and me were able to start up Atlantic Machines. Albert was always regarded as Angelo's trusted representative over here.

But, when it came to it, poor Angelo wasn't invincible. He was shot as he sat in his car after he'd had dinner in a restaurant in Little Italy, his bodyguard John Stanfa was wounded. Who actually did it was never known and it isn't even all that clear who ordered it. It may have been because Bruno was due to go in front of the New Jersey State Commission of investigation, and whatever the American mafia said about keeping quiet and codes of honour of silence, an awful lot of them had talked when they needed to. After all silence, particularly in other people, is golden.

4 April 1968

It was in Brixton I talked to James Earl Ray who was convicted of killing the civil rights leader Martin Luther King Jr outside the Lorraine, Memphis, motel on 4 April 1968. He was waiting to be extradited back for trial and they were holding him rather like in the condemned cell, with two ordinary cells knocked into one and a day and night guard. After the killing Ray had gone to Canada and then he came here on a Canadian passport. Apparently, he went off to Lisbon and came back intending to go on to Brussels and that's when they nabbed him

The authorities had an idea the black community was going to storm the prison and string him up. I don't know how they thought they was going to find their way around in the first place if they ever got in, but I suppose it made good newspaper stories. Nor could I see why, if they feared all this trouble, they didn't move Ray to some other prison where there wasn't any great number of blacks and they could hold him. But no one asked me. The screws didn't really like you talking to him but they was a bit leery of the whole thing and you could have a few words. He never said much about the case; not that he'd done it or he hadn't. All he said to me was that King was stirring up trouble for the whites.

It wasn't long before I had a fight with a principal screw in his office and I wasn't half ill after it. It was just the forerunner of what happened to me in Chelmsford years later. This time there was trouble with my letters. If the screws wanted they could always delay you getting them just to wind you up, because there was no way you get to a phone to ring up your family and see if anything was wrong, and they were having one of their clampdowns. I got knocked more or less unconscious. It was the usual procedure, get you down and then put you in a body belt – which was faster than putting you in a straitjacket. After that you were at their mercy. I got rushed over to the padded cell and got injected to put me out. The doctor must have had another mucky needle for it really done me completely. I was knocked out for days on end and then, after a bit, I was rushed over to Wandsworth in the van and put straight down the punishment block. It was there some screw took a look at me and told me I'd got jaundice. They wouldn't let Doreen or Eva in to see me in case they got infected and they caused ructions over it. Looking back they was a really good tag team. In fact they'd have made a good pair of coppers. Doreen was sweetness and light but tough and determined underneath – the DI Soft – and Eva was the aggressive one, the DS Hard. Nowadays I could probably have sued the Home Office but in them days there wasn't any question of that.

They flew Ray back to America handcuffed to that crooked copper Alec Eist, and lo and behold when they're halfway over the Atlantic he makes some sort of remark which looks like a sort of confession. Straight up verbal, I'd call it. All of a sudden Eist's a hero. It didn't stop him getting done later for a bit of corruption, but he got himself out of that. He then had some sort of business which was always going up in flames and then he bought a pub near Newmarket racecourse where he went and had a heart attack on the floor. I never did any business with him, but it was generally agreed he was the most bent copper in London at the time, and that was going something.

Once they'd got Ray back he pleaded guilty and got 99 years. I suppose it was a mercy that the death penalty was suspended but I wouldn't fancy that time in a prison in the South for killing a black leader. It's a wonder he's survived. Even better, he escaped in 1969 – but he didn't have any backing or anywhere to go. It's amazing he lasted the three days on the outside he did. From the moment he got the sentence he's been trying to get his conviction overturned all these years. Fat chance of that, but good luck to him. Some people say he wasn't the killer and, just like the Kennedy assassination, there's been all sorts of theories about who set it up and whether Ray really was on it. In fact there was some sort of civil case in America last year when the whole thing gets re-argued and the jury decided that Ray didn't do it. I think it was shown on the telly, and whilst Luther King's family has said it isn't sure it was Ray, I don't suppose that'll be enough to get him out.

5 April 1955

The story that the Krays were looking for me after the Spring Meeting at Epsom is utter rubbish. They're meant to have been protecting Jack Spot against me and Billy Blythe on the free course on the Downs. The story goes that Billy and me were in a pub in Islington and ready to fight it out but it's wrong. It's one of those bits of legend that's grown up about them. I don't think I was even on the Downs that day. If I was I never saw them.

I first met them when they were kids back around 1943. They'd be about nine then. I knew their dad, old Charlie, after I came out of Chelmsford and before I got the next lot. Remember there wasn't all that number of villains around then, and a lot of them were either inside or in the army, so even then I was a bit of a name. I used to go round his house for a cup of tea.

I think I first saw them at Brighton with Jack Spot. That's another racecourse looks just like Epsom, uphill, turn left, down a sort of Tattenham Corner and into the straight. People say that's where the Sabini fight was but they're wrong. It was at Lewes, which got closed down years ago. That's not to say there weren't some good fights at Brighton. There's a free course there as well and that's where a great number of the bookies' pitches were; and Spot used to try to organise who stood where and who paid what. Just like the Sabinis did twenty and thirty years earlier. This would be well before Spot's fight with Albert. I was just out of Broadmoor and Billy White from Southend, no relation to the Whites from Clerkenwell, drove me and Billy Blythe.

Spot had little George Wood, who was one of the best and who got a seven over the London Airport robbery, with him and that's when he sent him over to ask if me and Billy would be interested in going into a club with him. I said if it was just George of course I would, but then he said it would be Spot's money and that's when I said 'No thanks'.

17 April 1942

Jimmy Essex was a man with a bit of luck. He got done for murder twice and got out of it both times. The first was in April 1942 after a fight at a coffee stall. Charlie Ransford got eighteen months and Johnny Dobbs drew a year. Jimmy got three. When he come out in 1944 Jimmy went in the army. They picked him up at the prison gates but he was on his toes soon enough and he got nicked again the following March. He tried to break into a snouter's and got twelve months. He'd done about two or three when this Scotch guy at Leeds picked on him.

Jimmy's trouble was that his reputation had preceded him and there's always someone wanting to make his name at your expense. Outside your cell you had a board with a card stuck in it. On one side there was your name and how long you were doing, early release date and so on. When you turned it over there was the court you'd come from and what you'd been done for. It wasn't difficult to have a look and see what someone else was in for, and that's what did for Jimmy.

He'd got a decent job in the mailbag shop. He wasn't sewing. He just was cutting lengths of the sacking with a knife. The Scots bloke had a right go at him and then went after him with a tool. Jimmy just stuck the knife straight in him. Self-defence, really. He got ten years for that. It would have been January 1945 and he came out in the spring of 1952. He was out about ten months if that, and he got eight years for warehouse breaking. Tommy McGovern, the British boxing champion, give evidence saying what a good bloke Jimmy was but it didn't do much good. Then he got seven or eight in 1958 and this time they made it Preventive Detention. You had to have been up the road to Quarter Sessions or Assizes three times and be over thirty for that, so Jim was well qualified.

He's a year older than me; lives down in Kent nowadays. I met him first in approved school and we escaped together twice. There was a bit about him in the papers the other day, just sort of mentioned him. Mary Daly, an old brass he'd been friendly with when he was much younger, died and all sorts of people went to her funeral. She'd been written up in a book a few weeks earlier about how she had the biggest string of brothels in London – from one end of Gloucester Place to the other – she'd been at it for years. The man who wrote the book said he thought Jimmy had been married to her at one time but he never was.[1] Funnily, although I met Mary I didn't know she was on the game. She kept a low profile. In those days, the 50s that is, most of the birds on the game were on the street. Only the high class ones had flats. I was always polite to them. That's what saved me when I was done for slashing Bobby Ramsey the day Albert Dimes was acquitted over the Spot fight in August 1954. I knew the brass who was with him from Soho, and she said she was definite it wasn't me. Of course most of the showgirls in clubs like Churchills were on the game but they were classy brasses. They'd have been terribly offended if someone called them a prostitute. But if a

---

[1] Nick Davies, *Dark Heart* (1998) Vintage, London.

face went in then you'd buy the girls drinks, and not the stuff they served the punters, and she'd go home or to a hotel with you. If you left her a score that was up to you.

I knew Georgie Porritt well. He was another lucky one so far as topping goes. He was at Durham with me in the 1960s. In May 1961 he'd killed his stepfather and was very nearly topped for it. What had happened was George Porritt become involved with Florence 'Fluffy' Copeland, the former girlfriend of Cadillac Johnny Copley – his real name was Edwin – who was killed in a chase over Tower Bridge. The Copleys didn't really like her going with Georgie and a quarrel broke out in the Manor House Club, near Wrotham in Kent, between Mrs Copley and Fluffy. Later that night some people come round the Porritts' home and George, who always had a few guns stacked away, seeing two men attacking his stepfather, fired a shotgun. What he did was miss the men and kill his stepfather and they did him for murder – which was a topping offence with a firearm.

The jury recommended mercy and the Copleys did their bit, saying that the stepfather was the villain of it all, inciting Georgie to get the gun out, and I'm pleased to say it was a success. The Court said that although no one had suggested manslaughter as a defence the judge should have thought of it himself and Georgie got a ten. But there was a sadness because him and Fluffy broke up. Whilst he was on the Moor he married a girl called Sheila from Manchester, Abe Tobias's girl. A bit later she got done for being the driver on a bank job. She couldn't find a minder for her kid and she took it along on the raid. Later she found a minder for the evening and went and paid her £2 out of the stolen money and it got traced back. She did the job with one of the Reddans brothers from Canning Town and he got a ten.[2]

When I was turfed out of Dartmoor for organising a hunger strike I went to Durham and George had been moved there, more or less straight after his reprieve. When I got out I sent him £25 or £50 so he could buy himself a wireless or something like that. Anyway, only a couple of year ago one of my family was down in Scribes, the place Terry Venables owned in Knightsbridge, and Georgie give him £500 for me. After all them years he'd remembered. I met him at one of the Eubank–Benn fights and thanked him properly. He's doing well, I'm pleased to say, but poor old Bobby Ramsey died almost alone last year, out in an old people's home in Essex.

---

[2] George Porritt was convicted on 5 July 1961 and his appeal was allowed on the day before he was due to hang. Even though the defence had not raised the question of manslaughter the judge should have done so of his own volition, said the Court of Appeal. A sentence of 10 years' imprisonment was substituted.

24 April 1975

My boy Frank got chucked on the Bank of America job, the second one that is. That was a good job. The first, six months earlier, was a fiasco. The second one worked near enough to perfection. There was some really good men involved and one snake, Mickey Gervaise, who went on and became a supergrass. It all started out with a Stuart Buckley who'd just done a nine month, but despite this got a job in the Mayfair branch of the Bank of America in Davies Street. He had a key to carry out inspections and he knew some serious faces. They had some meets and a bit later Buckley took Leonard Wilde, who was known as Johnny the Boche – they called him that because he looked like a German – and who was a great man with keys and locks, down to the vault where the safeboxes were. He made some impressions of keys they'd found in a manager's drawer and set about doing a bit of recruiting. That is the sort of job where you need people with different talents. You want a bellman, someone who can cut the alarms, for a start. Then you've got to have a look-out man, some drivers, a slaughter to put the gear in and some soldiers. And you probably want some fences lined up. That's the trouble: the more you have the more you have to trust.

The first time they did it just about everything went wrong. They took in all the proper gear but drill bits began to overheat, then a couple of computer people turned up and, thank God the look-out, Billy Gear, spotted them but there was such a noise he couldn't make himself heard and he had to switch the power off. All that happened was the power which had been holding some magnets in place was cut and the drill they were holding broke on the floor. They waited till the guys had gone and started again, but more drills broke and they thought someone was telling them something and they pushed off.

Funnily enough it was Buckley who was sent to install a new alarm system, and when he was climbing up in the ceiling looking for a way to lead a power line he heard voices and realised he was looking at the vault door itself. It was then a question of watching the bank staff turn the locks and seeing what the combination was. Again they got interrupted, but this time they tied up the computer staff and it was reckoned they got away with over £8 million. Buckley got arrested the next day and started singing straight away. He said the reason he did this is he hadn't wanted no violence but a short sentence was more likely. But the coppers had also been watching the team for weeks. They went and dug up £120,000 down in Sussex where Buckley had buried his share.

There was some heavy bird handed out. Buckley got seven years but when it came to it he only did about two and a half. Mickey Gervaise, who by this time had become a supergrass, picked up 18 months and Billy Gear drew an 18 years. Johnny the Boche picked up 23 and Peter Colson a 21.

Anyway Frank Maple, who the coppers thought was the mastermind, got away, and by the time they found him and my boy Frank, Buckley wasn't so keen to give evidence and they both walked.

There was one famous woman who claimed she'd had her fur coat stolen and I think she had to go to court over it. I'm glad to say she won. My boy said he didn't see any fur coat in the boxes but that shows he should keep his eyes more open.

2 May 1965

Of those of us in the slashing of Jack Spot, the only one I keep in touch with nowadays is Battles Rossi. I see him regularly at the Italian Festival in Clerkenwell. He was one of those who wasn't even there, but who Spot decided to put in the frame. It had all come out of that fight he had with Albert Dimes. If he'd left it alone after that then it would all have been forgotten. Everyone would have tried to get both of them out because it was nothing to do with the law. But then Spot rents that little mug Joey Cannon from Paddington, which was Spot's area, to come and try to shoot Billy and Albert and we couldn't stand for that. I took his gun off of him and gave him a right talking to. But that's what did for Spot, and on top there were a number of others who were quite happy to see him done.

The best thing is he knew it was on top and he showed himself in his true light going running to Nipper Read and the other coppers, wanting them to protect him. But he wouldn't say who he wanted to be protected from, and even if he had there'd have been others. So we got the word he'd gone out for a meal and had left the caff and we was waiting for him when him and Rita come home that night, back to their flat off Hyde Park. Joey Cannon says he'd gone out with a bird and forgotten the time, so good for him. Jack got a right spanking and Joey'd have had one as well if he'd been there.

But as it was, Spot just put the bubble in. He and the Carters, who had it in for us, carved it up as to who they would say had tried to do them and who had done Spot. He went and put down me, which was right, and Bobby Warren who's uncle to Frank, the boxing promoter, which wasn't. Nor was Battles there. Dido Frett was there. Spot dropped him out and the Carters put him in for their bit of trouble. Billy Blythe was there, but when it came to it there was no need for him to do any of the work. I did it myself. Of course, he'd have joined in if there was any sign of trouble for me but there wasn't none at all.

Poor Billy's dead now. He died during the seven he picked up with me that time. He was a lovely man, God rest his soul. He come originally from Clerkenwell and he was about six or eight years older than me. He wasn't big. He was bald and he looked a bit frail but there was nothing weak about him except the ulcers he suffered from. That was what did for him; he couldn't get proper medical attention in the nick and one of them burst. Died in agony. He was one of the best. He could really have a row. He was a good thief and a good man to have with you. Billy and me and Gerry Newman did a bank job in North London during the war; not the actual bank just the usual. We took out the men on their way back to their offices to pay the wages. Billy was also useful with Albert Dimes at the Point-to-Points, but if you had to say what his speciality was it was cutting coppers.

Don't forget that during the war and a bit afterwards the coppers more or less had a licence. It's all very well having that famous photograph of the copper Peter Beveridge raising his hat when he's about to arrest that murderess, but that's not how it was when the coppers, like Tommy Butler and his mate Peter Vibart, were arresting the likes of us. They could drag you off the street, give you a back hander and, if they wanted, steam straight into you.

Vibart was an up-and-coming copper during and just after the war and he was a great drinker. In them days coppers and villains would drink together all the while, and one night him and Billy was in the pub and Billy cut him properly. It would be about 1946 or '47. He got three years' Penal Servitude for it and he thought it was worth it. You might think nowadays that three years was cheap for cutting a copper but three years then was really hard. No parole, no home leave. If a man got a five like my friend Patsy Lyons did – over the raid on a jeweller's in Victoria he and me and Johnny MacDonald did just after the war – it was the talk of the town. GBH on the law got you a stiff sentence but nowhere near as stiff as it would be today.

After Billy came out on ticket of leave from doing Vibart he picked up another three and they added on another twelve months from the previous. He knew of Billy Hill, of course, who didn't? But I introduced him so to speak in the nick when Hilly came in doing three years in 1947. Then when they both were out in 1950 Billy joined up with him. He was a gambler was Billy Blythe, brother-in-law of Harry Barham who was killed down on Hackney Marshes in 1972. That's how Billy made his living really, that and minding Stanley Baker's father-in-law down the markets.

Harry Barham was a good chap. Once, when it looked I was going to come unstuck after I'd done a tobacconist's, Harry was the one I got hold of and he came straight down and took the gear off of me. I don't really know that much about his killing. I do know Harry was in some trouble with tax and looked like he was going to get a good bit of bird at the Old Bailey. He'd been told if he pulled up money to pay some of the tax he'd stand half a chance of staying out so he went round Hatton

Garden buying jewellery on tick and then selling it at a loss straight off, just to get the cash.

He'd got quite a bit on him and he went and had a cup of tea in a caff in Red Lion Street, Holborn. That was more or less the last anyone see of him until he's found dead in the back of the car. And, of course, there's no cash to go with him. People said it was Teddy Machin, who was out of West Ham and who was one of Jack Spot's men. Teddy started sawing the legs off Jimmy Wooder at Ascot Races one day, and he was a hard man so he was fully capable of killing Harry – but I don't think he did.

But it was really Billy and not Harry that I was close to. So when I come out of Broadmoor the first piece of work I did I had him with me; and the second. Billy was gutted he missed the really big one we did at Christmas in Victoria Park in Hackney. We must have had sixty grand in a wages snatch when we got a hooky driver from the firm and clipped the bag off the wrist of a security man. The reason Billy wasn't on it was that it wasn't my job. If you found a job then you were the main man and it was up to you to say who was going to be on it. This one was picked up by Alfie Alpress so he had the say. I was amazed he didn't have Billy because he knew he was a good worker and he'd known him in Rochester Borstal before the war. Alfie hated Jack Spot. His sister was married to Charlie Dale, who Spot cut right across the nose. I was with Alfie when he did Solly Kankus, Solly the Yid, who was some sort of cousin of Spot. Knocked him spark out.

Poor Billy, he got seven years and he died in the nick in Liverpool in January 1958. Tragedy, he was such a good man, the best. He had a big funeral back in Clerkenwell. Eva went to it. I was in the nick down South at the time.

8 May 1959

One of the biggest rows about capital punishment came when Ronnie Marwood was hanged. He come from a good family and wasn't really one of the boys. He'd got just the one conviction for thieving when he was a kid and he was married with a young family. This was the day there was the fight at Gray's Dance Academy, a dance hall in the Holloway Road, near Highbury Corner, and he was meant to have stabbed a copper – Raymond Summers – who tried to break it up. Ronnie been done himself with a chopper before the copper arrived. The wrestler Bert Assirati was the doorman that afternoon and you might think he would have broken the fight up before it started, but that's easy to say when there are knives and coppers about. Bert wasn't any sort of coward, that's certain. There was one time someone stabbed him in the arm and despite the blood he was leaking he held on to him. Bert went on to work with that property owner Peter Rachman at his club in Soho, and then he went down to live in Brighton. By the end, all those bangs he took had an effect and he ended in a wheelchair. He died around 1970.

There's a lot who say it wasn't Ronnie Marwood who did the actual stabbing, but it was someone else who's gone on to become a TV star. The Nashes and Ronnie and Reggie hid him out for a time, but rather than cause them great aggravation he went and gave himself up in the New Year. In fact Ronnie and Reggie used to say that the troubles they had with the police began when they hid young Marwood.

It shows how quick the courts were in them days. The fight was on 13 December 1958. All the other kids were sent for trial by the end of the year, and remember in them days there was no thing like a quick committal. Every word – photographer, plan drawer and every witness had to have his evidence written down and read out. It took hours, but the beak at Clerkenwell had it through in no time.

Ronnie gave himself up in the January and he was hanged inside four months. The police said that he made a statement saying that when he saw one of his friends being arrested he'd stabbed the copper inadvertently, not knowing he was holding the knife. At his trial he said that was all wrong and that the coppers had just written down what they wanted and he'd signed it, not reading it because he'd been questioned on and off for thirteen hours and he was exhausted.

The jury wouldn't have it and Marwood got sentenced to death. There was a big rumpus and over 150 MPs signed a petition asking for a reprieve and Sydney Silverman, whose brother was a crook and did time with me, tabled a motion in the House of Commons. At that time we used to be out of our cells before an execution, but Jimmy Andrews and me and one or two others put buttons in the cell locks so they couldn't be shut the night before, and there was panic. There was also a ruckus in the prison the night before they topped Ronnie. I think that execution was the first one since, I would say, the beginning of the last century, where all the prisoners were locked in their cells. Before then, they'd been allowed out but after that everyone was banged up until maybe midday.

Outside the prison there was all sorts of trouble as well, and when the cinema newsreels played pictures of the crowd outside the prison the police were booed.

It was the second execution in ten days. There hadn't been one for something like five years and everyone was very edgy. The previous guy's case had been a bit of a funny one as well. In fact it was a bit like the Craig and Bentley case. A young bloke called Pritchard turned QE on a man named Joseph Chrimes, who was done for the murder of a widow, Norah Summerfield. She'd surprised them in a burglary and the Pros' case was that Chrimes took out a tyre lever and battered her to death. The pair of them took a few things from her home.

Pritchard said he tried to stop his mate and Chrimes said it was Pritchard who was hitting the woman with the lever. The jury must have been a bit suspicious because they wanted to know why no evidence had been offered by the Pros against Pritchard and the judge told them it was a bit technical. Chrimes said he shouldn't have been convicted on the uncorroborated evidence of Pritchard, but the Court of Appeal said there was plenty of evidence against him. Funnily, Chrimes had only got one previous and that was for theft when he was fifteen.

What the real row was about was that a couple of months later there was another kid, Terence Cooney, who had been in a fight in a dance hall down the East End and had gone and stabbed someone from another firm. There was a real old set-to about why he was only convicted of non-capital murder and so got life, whilst Ronnie gets topped. It wasn't difficult to understand.

Then even the biggest mug, even one who wasn't one of the chaps – the sort of person we'd call a hearthrug – must realise that if you killed a copper someone had to swing for it. Even before they had that capital and non-capital murder difference, if you stabbed an ordinary geezer then you'd be in with half a chance and if you got it, good luck. Nobody inside would have the needle. Outsiders wouldn't understand. The police traded on it. It was a form of blackmail on whoever was Home Secretary. Look at Derek Bentley six years earlier – same thing.

Years earlier there had been another big row when Ronnie True got let off and a young boy called Henry Jacoby was topped. True had killed a brass and he was well connected in society so he went to Broadmoor. Jacoby was a pantry boy or something like it in a hotel, and he killed an old lady who had some title or other when he screwed her room. He went to the gallows and there was a terrible rumpus about that, with people saying it was one law for the rich and another for the poor.[1]

Once the topping was over the prison did the burying in the grounds. There was no such thing as burial duty for the prisoners. In Wandsworth there was a small garden with a wall round it. Prisoners never got near it, except Patsy Lyons got through it one day when he was nearly over the wall. After they nicked him he told me it was very neat. If he hadn't taken the time to admire it he might have been away.

---

[1] Ronald True was convicted on 5 May 1922 of the murder of Olive Young, also known as Gertrude Yates. He was reprieved and sent to Broadmoor where he became a member of their concert party and where he died aged sixty. It was said that his reprieve was due to the fact that he was the illegitimate son of the First World War General Sir John French but he was not that man's son. The 18-year-old Henry Julius Jacoby, who was convicted of the murder of Lady Alice White on 14 March 1922, was hanged on 7 June that year, despite a strong recommendation by the jury for mercy.

9 May 1968

This was a historic day. It was when Nipper Read and his men arrested the Twins and most of the rest of the Firm. Ronnie and Reggie had been out on the town the night before with the American Joey Kaufman, who was dealing in stolen bonds with them, and Nipper got them the next morning when they were in bed at their flat in the East End.

I first heard it in Leicester. Me and Tommy Wisbey, Bobby Welsh, Buster Edwards and Joey Martin were on the exercise yard and there was a Red Band used to collect rubbish and come and talk to us a bit. He wasn't supposed to, but he was a nutter and the screws let him alone. He calls out 'The Craigs are nicked. All of them'. I thought he meant the Craigs as in Craig and Bentley who got topped for doing the copper. Young Craig got life and had been out a few years then. His brother Neville had done some good bird in his time and for a minute I thought this old boy was talking about them. But when we got inside everyone knew.

It wasn't a surprise really. After us and Mr Smith's Club the Twins should have known the rats would come out of the woodwork. Then Frank Mitchell and Jack 'The Hat', and the fact that Ronnie had shot Georgie Cornell in the Beggar – they were open secrets. You can't expect to go round shooting people in public and not expect the whole world to know within five minutes. It was really just a matter of time. I remember thinking 'Poor sods, they're going to face the same problems as we did'.

13 May 1977

It was Jimmy Humphreys brought down the Porn Squad but, although I didn't know it at the time, in a way I helped.

I knew Jimmy Humphreys because he was a local boy; came from Southwark and he's a few years younger than me. He'll be about seventy now; very presentable, smart dresser, a very good appearance. Did all the usual things, a bit of approved school, a bit of burglary. In fact he and I got chucked in 1951 when we were done for the screwing at the Howard Hotel in Aldwych, when we were trying to raise some money for Jackie Rosa[1] who was up for hitting a screw at Pentonville. We only got away with it because the police tried to stitch us up, leaving a copy of our convictions in the jury room so they'd know we'd got form. One of the

---

[1] Jack Rosa, one of a pair of brothers of Turkish extraction who came from the Elephant and Castle, had a long and distinguished criminal career. He took part in an attack on a prison officer in which Billy Hill intervened and 'saved' the warder. For this Billy received kudos and remission. Rosa, who that morning had received the cat-o'-nine-tails, blamed this aberration on the flogging and was not punished further. He received a substantial reward from Hill. He was one of a number of men attracted to Fay Richardson, known as the Black Widow because of their early deaths. Rosa was one. Fatally injured in a car crash and in possession of a false driving licence his dying words are said to have been 'I wasn't driving'.

jurors was from the East End and he didn't think it was fair, so he talked the others into a not guilty. Then Humphreys got six years in March 1958 for some postal orders down in Glamorgan.

When my sister Eva got married and was living in Great Dover Street he and his first wife June were down on their luck and Eva, through the kindness of her heart, had them and the baby to stay for about four months until they got on their feet. He wasn't a bad fellow then. A good thief until he broke up with June and after that he went bad.

I'm in Liverpool in 1958 and I used to have the *South London Press*. By now, you were allowed your local weekly paper and as that came out twice a week I was allowed both editions. I came across this story about a man who'd been found with a gun or a knife in his pocket – I forget which – and he'd said that Jimmy Humphreys had planted it and then shopped him. Truth is, I didn't think much of the man for saying that, but then I met Jimmy also in Liverpool three years later and he told me he had actually planted it. He must have been working with the Bill all that time. I never saw him after 1974 and I heard he went on protection.

But what happened about the Porn Squad was that when Humphreys come out of the Glamorgan bird he set up a drinker in Old Compton Street and he met up with an old girlfriend June Gaynor, known as 'Rusty'. Once she'd been a barmaid, but then she became a dancer and took her name from that Mitzi Gaynor and now she was taking her clothes off. Whilst Jimmy had been absent June had an affair with another Soho face, Peter 'Pookey' Garfath. She started working for Humphreys. Six months later they married.

You have to remember in the 1950s and 1960s in Soho the police more or less had a licence to do what they wanted and to blag who they wanted. One of the worst was that Harry Challenor, who liked to be called Tanky because he'd been in the Tank Corps in the war. In all fairness he'd been a brave man back then, but now he was taking money and fitting people up as well – which is the worst combination there is in a copper.

It was on his advice that Humphreys moved his club to Macclesfield Street. Humphreys wasn't only paying money to Challenor he was also his grass. Humphreys had been paying protection money to Challenor as well as providing him with tidbits of information on Soho life. Humphreys was a double dealer as well, because once he was in Macclesfield Street and Challenor asked for more money Humphreys paid him over two lots of £25 – and then made a complaint to the Commissioner. Of course it came to nothing. Complaints by toe-rags like Humphreys against brave and honest officers never got much further than the out tray.

In fact Challenor done him a good turn. Rusty wasn't only a good-looking woman and a good stripper she was a good businesswoman as well and the Macclesfield Street Club done well. Then she heard of premises in Walker Court, off Brewer Street, and had Humphreys open another club. She couldn't hardly have chosen better. For a start it was in the heart of Soho. Secondly, it was opposite Raymond's Revue Bar, which was where all the out of town punters went. Within a year they were rich.

What happened next was he teamed up with porn dealer Bernie Silver, who was paying the police protection. Humphreys wanted to open a dirty book shop in Rupert Street, but a man called Moody – who was then in charge of the Obscene Publications Squad which was the real name of the Porn Squad – wouldn't let him. So what do they do but have a Christmas lunch with him and Commander Wally Virgo at the Criterion in Piccadilly. Of course a deal was made, but when it all came out at the trial it was staggering. Something like £14,000 straight to the cozzers and then £2,000 a month to make sure there were no raids. Then Silver went abroad and

Humphreys, who was always a ladies' man, started having it away with Silver's number one girl, Dominique Ferguson. Silver got the hump and there was a time when it seemed like Humphreys was going to be fitted up. As it turned out Commander Ken Drury, whose father I knew all the way back at the beginning of the war when he was glad to have a tenner off me, sorted it all out – but apparently it cost Humphreys over a grand.

Of course it all started to unravel. In 1971 the *Sunday People* had started to make inquiries and made allegations in the paper about Silver and Humphreys and how they had dealings with corrupt officers. There was a sort of investigation but it came to nothing. You'd have thought after that scare the coppers would have had the sense to let it go, but in them days they could no more believe they'd be caught than they could fly. So they went at it another year and the paper kept on digging. Then it all came on top in a very funny way.

What happened was that Freddie Sewell was on his toes for killing that copper up in Blackpool after a blag which went wrong and they gave a spin to Joey Pyle's place. There was nothing to link him to Sewell but what there was, they said, was a gun and some ammo. Joey of course said they'd put it there, something which the judge pooh-poohed, saying that if they acquitted him it would mean the police had committed perjury – but the jury went and did just that. After that Joey got the hump with the Met in general and told the papers how Humphreys had taken Drury on holiday in Cyprus.

Drury tried to talk his way out, saying first that he'd paid his whack and when that didn't work, that he'd had a tip off that Ronnie Biggs was there and he was looking for him on his own time. Humphreys supported him, but this time the top brass realised they had to be doing a bit more and Drury was suspended. Then he did a really stupid thing. He went and sold his story to the

News of the World for ten grand, saying that Humphreys was a grass – which of course was right – and he'd been paying him money, which of course he wasn't. Now Humphreys really got the hump saying that he wasn't a grass and it was the other way round. It was Drury who'd been blagging money off him.

They got that Gilbert Kelland to do an investigation and he got hold of Rusty Humphreys's diaries. She just come out of Holloway because she'd been found with a gun. Now they started investigating how Pookey Garfath came to be slashed in the lavatory in the Dauphine Club in Marylebone. He said it was all down to Humphreys and it was a warning to stay away from Rusty when she came out of the nick. It was a fine old mess, because then Humphreys said the whole thing was a fit-up against him because Drury had had to resign. Then Pookey said the only reason he'd given evidence was that he was afraid if he hadn't put Humphreys away he'd have been dead in a year. He was. People said it was an overdose.

Humphreys got eight years for the Pookey slashing and he wanted out and so he started to talk to Kelland's team. Of course he wasn't going to be seen as very reliable and they weren't sure just what he was saying. What he was doing was naming high-up names like Commander Wally Virgo. So this was where I come in. At one time Virgo had been seconded as chief of prison security. At the time I was in Leicester. I didn't know it but Virgo was trying to get in touch with Humphreys and told him the authorities knew I was going to have a knife smuggled in on a visit, stab the governor and smuggle the knife out. Virgo also told him that all my visits were being tape-recorded. All he wanted was to blag a few quid off Humphreys and my family by acting as a so-called friend. In fact I'd never met Virgo. There'd been no need. One-arm bandits were legal so there was no question of needing a licence from him.

Even if I'd wanted to do it I couldn't. I was always surrounded by screws and in those days there was no touching no nothing; anyway they'd installed electronic equipment you had to pass through at the prison gates. I couldn't have been given anything at all. Not that either my wife Doreen, who was a straight girl, or Eva would have done it for me. They'd have known I would be caught and get into even more trouble and they'd have wanted to protect me from myself.

Anyway Jim did get a message to me and he contacted Eva. Something was up because when Eva and Doreen got to the prison they were marched into the governor's office where there's a screen and they were told they wouldn't be allowed to see me unless they agreed to a strip search. Quite rightly they never agreed and the visit was cancelled so they went straight down to the local paper, the *Leicester Mercury*, and to their credit they published the story. Then they went to the post office and sent me a telegram saying why they hadn't been in.

How it helped Humphreys was they checked up his story and they found Virgo had been in touch with him, telling him about the knife.

The Porn Trial was really big. In fact it was three trials in all. Humphreys got in a sulk and wouldn't give evidence in the first trial so they relied on another porn dealer, John Mason – no relation of the Eric Mason that I took an axe to. In fact it looked as though Humphreys was going to be upstaged and that must have hurt his pride and his chances of early release so he give evidence against Virgo and Moody. On 13 May 1977 they went down. He and Moody both got twelve years and Humphreys got a Royal Pardon for his good work.

After the trial I remember meeting a man in Cardiff. He was doing three years and Virgo got ten. For some reason he'd been sent early on to Leyhill, which was an open prison and not the sort of place you'd normally find someone in the first months of an eight-year sentence – unless you were a senior copper, that is. Virgo was telling this man he was confident he'd be chucked on appeal. It was almost as if he knew something. It was like, 'I don't mind that much getting a guilty but if I'm not out on appeal I'm going to really say something'. He did get out on the appeal. They said that the judge hadn't got the direction on what was corroboration right.[2] He died a few years later. Drury got eight years and he died in 1984.

Jimmy and Rusty Humphreys more or less stayed together. He went to Ireland and started training and breeding greyhounds near Knocklong in Limerick. He was keen on the dogs but he was also using the place to manufacture amphetamines. From what I heard he'd given the gardai so many good tips on the dogs someone did him the favour about the raid and he was off just in time. Then they went to America. From what I heard he got ripped off in some drugs deal and eventually they came back to London, where they started poncing, running girls from flats around Marylebone. You know the sort of thing: £20 for a hand job upwards. They even had one girl called herself Nurse Diana who was to give enemas. In July 1994 he got twelve months and Rusty got eight. The judge said they'd cleared £100,000 in twenty months which can't have been bad.

After that you heard talk of them doing a book and then the last I heard was there was going to be a film about Rusty's life, with that Ginger Spice playing her. But you hear all sorts of things about films. Good luck to her if it comes off.

Personally I couldn't have done what Humphreys done, not even to a copper. The only way I could have done it was if it could let out some poor sod who's been convicted – especially if the poor sod's innocent.

---

[2] Commander Virgo's conviction was quashed on 14 March 1978. See *The Times Law Report*.

There again when that screw in Wakefield, Hamilton, sent that disgusting card, absolute filth, to my sister Eva one Christmas I said I wouldn't give evidence against the other screws who'd been in on it. I did give them a bit of stick though. Every time I saw them I'd call out 'You're the ones' and there was nothing they could do about it. Nor did I give evidence against Hamilton. He pleaded guilty, said he was frightened of me, and he was quite right to be. If I'd of found out what he sent to Eva I'd have killed him.

21 May 1952

This was the day Billy showed his true mastery. The Eastcastle Street Post Office job. He was years ahead of his time. Once he'd plotted it all out he had his men in, briefed them and locked them all up until it was time to go. He trusted them but he just wanted to make double sure there could be no leaks. It was like he'd learned from those wartime slogans 'Be like Dad and keep mum' and 'Careless talk costs lives'. The copper Nipper Read learned that from him when he nicked the Krays, but Bert Wickstead made the mistake of letting his men loose once and, by the time the raid took place, it was all over the papers. Coppers are the same as everyone else. They'll do things for a bit of dough or a bit of kudos. Look at the copper who had the papers in to photograph the capture of George Davis when he did the Bank of Cyprus. The copper said the police had been having a bit of bad publicity and he wanted to give them a gee!

Anyway Billy got the Eastcastle Street job through his spieler in Soho. He had a man from the post office come in and play and the man got out of his depth. Billy could be wicked with cards. Him and that Charlie Taylor together. He was gambling good money and that's how Albert and Billy got to him. 'Give us the info and we'll let you off the debt'. Otherwise you got the info where you could. People would come with jobs they just wanted to share or they wanted to do but couldn't put a team together theirselves.

What the putter-up got out of it would depend. If it was ordinary then there'd be a drink but a drink could run to several hundred. If it was a good job then he'd get his full whack. There'd be no payment to someone to steal a motor for you. I know it happens today, but then you did it yourself and there was one less person knew about things. Getting someone to do it was asking for trouble.

What Bill had done was have the mail-van followed every night for months as it left on its journey to Oxford Street. Cars had been stolen specifically for the raid. As the van turned into Eastcastle Street off Oxford Street, two cars they had had nicked blocked the driver's path. In the early hours of Wednesday morning they'd disconnected the alarm system on the van whilst the staff were on their tea-break. They had the van and watched as it went to Paddington Station. Once it left there there was a call to the flat and they were after it.

As the van turned into Eastcastle Street the two cars blocked the driver's path. They did the three post-office workers, left them on the pavement and drove off. Even Bill would admit he couldn't have done it without Slip Sullivan's contacts in Smithfield, because the proceeds were driven about the East End in lorries belonging to market traders until Hilly decided it was safe for them to be unloaded.

The money was hidden in Jack Gyp's wholesale fruit lorry – Sonny Sullivan was his minder. It then went to another one of his lorries with sacks of potatoes and fruit all around it, and it went to Spitalfields and was parked with his other lorries before it was taken to the Borough, then Covent Garden, on to Stratford, and back to Spitalfields and round again until Bill decided it was safe to unload.

That was the thing with Bill. People didn't query his judgement and they was right not to. Others would not have listened and split the money before it was safe but not Bill. He had all good men who kept their mouths shut. Billy picked his people well. He didn't mind who worked with him either. People say he had that black man Charlie Spring from Regent's Canal Docks do a bit of the driving. The story is he moved twenty grand or so down to Kent and he got caught with a bit of it. They never traced it back and Charlie was a good man. He stayed stumm and Bill give him a grand and his wife a pension of £20 a week for the six months he was away. I don't know if it's true, because I was away and Bill never mentioned it to me. Not that there was any need for him to. In those days, or today for that matter, you don't find too many mixed teams so to speak.

There was big rewards on offer but they were never claimed. What a contrast to the London Airport job.

Poor Sonny, he got done with a carving knife a few years later. For a bit there was all sorts of stories going round that there was going to be gang wars over it. Billy had to sort that out as well. In fact it was his wife, a Polish girl with a great temper, that did it. Billy arranged that Sonny should see his brother Slip just as he was dying and, lo and behold, Sonny tells him it was an accident. That's what the inquest jury returned. Sonny got a big send off and Slip was alive until a few years ago. Lived over the East End but he was in poor health a lot of the time. He gave me a bell just after my first book came out but I'm sorry I never went over to see him like I should.

31 May 1964

This was one of the best days in prison ever. It was the day they abolished bread and water as a punishment. That was a really big plus. Before then the screws were on a high when they give you just this lump of bread. And the lump would be a right bit of rubbish, something they should have slung away a couple of days previous. If you'd had a camera you could have had a picture of them gloating. They'd have a conversation in front of you to rub it in. 'What you having tonight then, Harry?' 'The missus has got a bit of steak, we'll be having that'.

By now things were getting a bit better all round. Not that the screws were, but things you could do. The screws themselves were in collar and tie instead of high collars. That had started to come in about 1949. What they wanted was to be like coppers who'd been out of those collars by the end of the war. Screws were really jealous of coppers. That's why if a man was ordered to have a flogging for something outside, the screws didn't lay it on as thick as you could have expected. They were thought of as second-class. Even the Bobby had a good friendly image in them days. 'If you want to know the time, ask a policeman'. The screws had nothing like that.

It was round about 1949 we started to get tea at teatime. Up until then it was tea for breakfast and cocoa at teatime. Then we started to get cocoa of an evening. Then the screws would give you a little metal cup of brown sugar for your cocoa and your morning tea and porridge. Of course, if the screws didn't like you and you'd just come up from the punishment block you'd find yourself in the end cell, getting served last of all. By now your toke of bread would be falling to pieces and the cocoa would just be skin and slime off the bottom of the urn.

In a morning they'd unlock you and so many of you at a time could go to the wash recess and throw your slops away. You'd get a wash in cold water at the same time. About the first job I ever had in the nick was to go with a screw and bring up boiling water for shaving. You had to. I could get away with it because I've got a smooth skin, but men with heavy beards could go without a day or so and then it was on report. You did this in your cell. It would be with one of them old-fashioned blades like you cut balsa with when you was a kid. You were meant to have your own marked with your cell number, but you never did. You had to hand it in when you were finished. As for getting a new blade, maybe every Pancake Tuesday. I'd hold the water and the screw would ladle it out into a shaving mug, but very often there wasn't one and it went in your tea mug.

Of all the things, mailbag sewing was the worst. It was with you perpetually. You had to do three or four after breakfast, after dinner and after tea at four o'clock in your cell. Some people used to gamble on doing all theirs in the evening. But it was a gamble because dead on eight o'clock, or a bit after, the lights went out. They come on again about six and that gave you a chance to catch up if you was behind. At the weekend you got extra and this was on top of what you did in the shop. It's funny they let you keep your needle overnight, and also your tin knife for cutting the thread and marging your bread.

You could be putting the rope around the top, or you'd do the top or the bottom; eight stitches or more to an inch. More men must have lost remission over that than any other single discipline offence; even more than talking in the shop. Prisons were almost empty and the screws had plenty of time to make sure you were doing your sewing right.

Another good day was in 1946 when the Governor at Liverpool announced that because of shortages mailbag sewing was going to be suspended. That was wonderful. They tried to bring it back in 1953, but the cons weren't standing for it and they had to abandon the idea after about three weeks.

During the war there was a rule that anyone with three years' penal servitude could do it in a local prison, but quite a lot of prisoners petitioned to go to the Moor where there were little privileges like association.

As for letters, until 1949 it was once a month in and out, and you couldn't write a letter for your first eight weeks. You couldn't have a visit for your first eight weeks either. They really wanted to make sure you had a stable home life.

Radios came in eventually. Preventive detention came in April 1949, after the Criminal Justice Bill the previous year. It was really the same as corrective training. You had to be of sound mind, be over thirty and have three convictions up the steps. Then it would never be less than a five and a seven was usual. It's amazing when you think not all that long before an average sentence for a robbery was a year and twelve strokes of the cat. Once a con got to a long-term nick he could have his radio. If you weren't doing PD you had to do four years from the date of your sentence before you got a radio. Time on remand didn't count. So if you got a six and didn't lose remission you were out in four and so you never had a radio. You might think that PD was an advantage, but the trouble was that at the start you only got a sixth remission instead of a third. It went out around 1968.

The screws didn't like you having radios at first, same as they didn't like prisoners seeing the telly. They'd put you on report for having it on too loud and they wanted the governors to authorise confiscation of the radios for offences – but to their credit they wouldn't do it.

Being a young prisoner wasn't any fun in the 1930s and '40s. Even on remand you had to do PT in a little vest and shorts and sort of clogs with the nails coming through. They were made in prisons up and down the country and they were really the same as boots. I remember old Patsy Lyons at Feltham not doing his exercises as the screw wanted and they got in a fight. In those days if you assaulted a screw you were taking your life in your hands.

That was the only formal training I ever did. People didn't go in for fitness in those days. You played a bit of football at school, but after that nothing until I was in the Soho Rangers football team which was managed by Stanley Baker. I kept fit in prison by just walking up and down my cell day in and night out. Every so often I'd do a few press-ups but it was really just walking. I remember that old pro boxer Jimmy Ford, he'd been at Dunkirk and he was with me in Lewes. Even when he was fighting he didn't train. Mind you he was fighting say three times a fortnight, and possibly more, so he really did his training in the ring. He did a screw in Lewes and got the cat for it.

Later on in my sentences they got a few weights into the prisons. The screws didn't like it a bit and tried to resist, just as they tried to resist all progress. They said the weights could be used for escaping. There weren't any gyms at this stage. The weights were just on the landing but I never used them. I didn't want to give the screws half a chance to laugh at me. They'd stand there watching people struggle to lift them and they'd half smirk when they couldn't. I wasn't having them do that at me so I kept to my walking.

It was only the dogs of the screws who wanted to be on the punishment block. They fought for the privilege. It was easy work; we had to slop out one at a time. There was more screws than there was prisoners. Nine-tenths of the prisoners down there would be nonces or grasses on Rule 43 and they'd be fawning over them, cleaning the screws' room, making them a bit of tea and toast, frying eggs for them so we could smell it. People don't realise the brooding, the evilness of it all for the rest of us. It made you realise the next stop for the screws would be Dachau and they'd have had no qualms.

You read now about all the sex there is in prisons and about whether there should be condoms handed out so that once people come out they don't infect their wives and girlfriends. Personally, I think that's a good idea but there was no need for it in my day. Of course there wasn't AIDS, but there wasn't much sex either. Parkhurst, on the Island, was where the feeble-minded prisoners got sent before the war and I suppose it was there where there was most of it. There's stories that some people made rouge out of mailbags and put margarine in their hair to make them little kiss curls and that one prisoner had an affair with a screw, but if they did I never saw it. I suppose there was one or two obvious ones in each prison but no more. Apart from anything else there wasn't much opportunity. There weren't no showers. Bathing was done in a big open room with maybe ten baths in it and the screws walking up and down between them. There wasn't all that much association and everyone had his own cell. For most of us it was a question of Widow Palm.

1 June 1957

I was in the High Court in the Strand this day. It was all a spin-off from Jack Spot and his fight with Albert Dimes and the slashing I gave Spot as a result. After what Spotty and his wife Rita did to Battles Rossi and Bobby Warren, putting them there with me when they were miles away, Billy Hill decided to treat him the same way. So he fixed it that he got accused of attacking Big Tommy Falco and putting forty-seven stitches in him outside the Astor Club. Tommy said he heard Spotty say 'This is one for Albert' and Johnny Rice, who was Albert's driver, gave evidence that he'd heard Spotty say the same thing.

I have to admit it wasn't Bill's finest hour involving the police as he did. But if he'd had Spot cut up again then there's no knowing which innocent man him and Rita might have named. Anyway Spot had an answer to this one. What had happened was that Billy Hill had offered Victor Russo, who was known as 'Scarface Jock', £500 to allow himself to be slashed so Spot could be put in the frame. It wouldn't have made his mug that much uglier because people had been having a go at it for some time. There'd been a meeting in a back room in Peter Mario's in Gerrard Street, along with the crime reporter Duncan Webb, and one of the questions which had come up was how they could make sure that Spot didn't have a cast-iron alibi. What they'd decided was that they'd get Sid Kiki the bookmaker, who was also a police grass, to find out where Spot was that night. Russo turned it down and so Tommy Falco took his place. But Russo wouldn't stand for it when he heard Spot had been arrested. He told Hill he was going to the police. That's what he did and the end of it was that Spot got chucked.

Then whilst I was doing my seven for slashing Spot in the first place, the *Empire News* – which was a Sunday rag rather like the *News of the World* – wrote an article with a headline YARD STARTS NEW SPOT TRIAL PROBE and saying that a statement had been taken from me in Lincoln prison. What this meant, of course, was that I was grassing someone and I wasn't having it. They did offer me a few quid to settle and get rid of me, because even if they won there was no question of getting any costs out of me. In the meantime, I was having a grand old time, what with getting visits to discuss the case, and so I turned it down.

Eva had a whip and got me those West End solicitors Bellamy Bestford to act. They acted in a lot of big cases in them days until the old man died and the son got struck off. The solicitor's clerk, Brian Field, who got done in the Great Train Robbery, come to see me in Liverpool to ask me about settling but I wasn't having any. He was the one that bought Leatherslade Farm for the Train hide-out.

The end result is that I've got my case before Mr Justice Slade and a jury with John Platts Mills, who went on to defend Ronnie Kray, representing me. We called a screw who produced records which proved there'd been no visit to me by the police. Then I got in the witness box and that Helenus Milmo – who went on to be a judge and who was acting for the paper – asked me if a law-abiding citizen would think any the worse of me if it was known I'd helped the police. I said I wouldn't know what would be in an honest person's mind and he said he could quite understand that. Laughter in court. His defence was that even though what they'd printed was false it couldn't be libel to say I'd discharged my duty as a law abiding citizen. And that's what the jury said as well. They weren't out half an hour. But I had a day out and it was worth it to show I hadn't grassed anyone.

Overall, criminals don't do too good in court. In many ways it's ruined a number of them. Old Darby Sabini from Clerkenwell didn't do himself any favours before the war when he sued some tuppenny ha'penny paper for saying he headed a racecourse gang. He didn't turn up for the hearing and the end result was they made him bankrupt. Jack Spot got in trouble with the reporter Duncan Webb. He didn't sue him but he broke his arm and had damages awarded against him. Then the Great Train robbers tried to sue that writer Peta Fordham, whose husband Wilfrid defended a lot of them, over what she'd written in the book *The Robbers' Tale*, but that didn't do them much good.

In fact the only one who did any good whatever was Alfie Hinds. He was really lucky. I'd known Alfie a long time because he grew up near where I lived. His father had the cat after a big bank robbery in Portsmouth and he never really recovered. It was his mother's fault her old man got nicked. After the raid she went around the Elephant wearing pussies, and it was only a matter of time before someone put two and two together and bubbled.

Alfie was a good thief, a safebreaker and they're hard to come by, but he was a mean man and in 1953 he got done for the Maples safebreaking in Tottenham Court Road. He was arrested down on the Thames some place by a copper, Herbert Sparkes, who said that dust from Maples could be traced in his trouser turn-ups. Alfie yelled blue murder and said his trousers had been cleaned and he hadn't worn them since. He didn't get on with his brief and he was unlucky because the man never called some alibi witnesses Hinds wanted. What he said was that Sparkes had planted the dust and that wasn't something which appealed to the judge, who was that pig Goddard, or the jury in them days. Police officers didn't do things like that then.

In fairness Alfie had been in the wrong place at the wrong time. On the Monday prior to the theft he had gone to Tottenham Court Road to buy a carpet in a pub. He had lent the man his Land Rover and when it had not been returned had telephoned the police and reported it stolen. The man was one of those nicked with Alfie. His argument went that if he had been on the job he wouldn't have done such a thing. The Pros said that the counter-argument was that this was a diabolically cunning move to divert suspicion if his vehicle had been seen on a reconnoitre. Down he went for a twelve. Alfie kept on protesting his innocence but it didn't do him any good. He also kept on escaping which, in its way did, because he was forever in the papers and everybody loves a rascal. There was never any suggestion he was up to villainy whilst he was on his toes and people liked him.

It was the fashion in those days that when coppers retired they wrote their memoirs either in a book like Fabian or, if they weren't as famous, at least in a Sunday paper and that's what Sparkes did. He wrote that Alfie should stop whining and take his medicine like a man and Alfie, who was now on the hostel scheme, sued him for libel and he pulled a really good stroke. To show what a sport he was he offered to withdraw the case if he could have his appeal re-opened. Of course, the authorities weren't having anything of that.

This time he was much better prepared and was represented by James Comyn, who was later to become a High Court judge himself. Comyn called experts to throw cold water over the scientific evidence. Alfie's alibi witnesses stood up and he came over much better to the jury than emotional Sparkes who kept getting very upset in the box. When he was being cross-examined, Alfie was also fortunate because the case of that crooked copper Tanky Challenor had not been forgotten and, when at one point during the cross Sparkes buried his face in his hands, someone in the gallery called 'Watch out! He's doing a Challenor'.

Of course the judge wasn't having it and he was dead against Alfie but the jury went for him and give him a bit over a grand. Then old Alfie goes one better and goes back to the Court of Appeal to have his conviction quashed. Comyn advised him not to but he would go ahead. But the Court of Appeal isn't a jury and they turned him down flat. So there he is acquitted by a jury and convicted by a jury. It doesn't matter to him. He was out by now and talking on the criminal justice system at polytechnics. He did change the law, however, because a rule was brought in so that if you had a criminal conviction you couldn't bring civil proceedings to claim it was wrong. Later Alfie made a fortune with his old friend Tony Maffia and went off to the Channel Islands where he was a successful property developer.

I think the truth is that Alfie was on the job and Sparkes knew it and put the dust in his turn-ups. As for the car, what had happened was that it had been nicked by Freddie Sewell who went on to kill a copper. Alfie was so mean he hadn't put any oil in the engine and it had blown up after a couple of streets and Sewell had to abandon it.

Despite what people say Alfie never gave up crime. At one time he was acting as the intermediary over here for that gang of robbers in Melbourne they called the Toe Cutters. He died a few years ago.

11 June 1976

This was the day Jackie O'Connell got himself shot and I mean that literally. I knew his cousin Frank much better but Jackie was a good thief, a good safebreaker. He was regarded as a very lucky man in his day. Like I say, most of us could spend hours doing a safe and find there was nothing in it. Jackie could go in a place and find not only that there was all the takings in it but they'd left the door unlocked to go with it.

He got done for the first Bank of America job, the one that failed, and he'd been grassed up by Buckley, the inside man. Now he'd got Billy Rees-Davies, the one-armed MP, defending him, same as I was meant to have for the Parkhurst Trial. The day Jackie is going to court he arranges that someone will shoot him so he doesn't have to stand trial with the others and is going to get a bit of sympathy. Unfortunately what happens is the guy Jackie's hired gets too close and the result is Jackie loses his leg same as Happy Sambridge did when I'd finished with him. But what's worse is Jackie's paid for it to happen. It took him out of the main trial and when he eventually goes to court about a year and a half later it got him a reduced sentence of course. The brief said he'd led a blameless life for many years, but he was in a lot of pain afterwards. It seems like even though there's no leg you get phantom pains. That's what Jackie did and eventually he couldn't stand it and went and topped himself.

He was well out of the main trial. They were handing out twenty-ones and twenty-threes that day. Make sure you can't enjoy the proceeds, said the judge. Johnny the Boche had picked up the twenty-three and Peter Colson twenty-one; Billy Gear got eighteen years and Mickey Gervaise the grass got eighteen months. He'd already been nicked on other things by this time.

When I say Jackie was lucky I mean it. Well, in 1965 or '66 long before the Bank of America he and his cousin Frank had a little tickle going with the Express Dairy in Wood Green, a couple of hundred yards from the tube station it was. A Saturday afternoon blag when all the Christmas takings would be there. A couple of weeks before the off Jackie gets done for driving whilst disqualified. In those days it was regarded as much more serious than it is today and it was three months inside regular. That's what he got. Appealed to Quarter Sessions and they said stay where you are and so he missed the raid. It was just as well for Jackie because Joey Martin went to replace him.

The takings were being counted in an office upstairs above the yard and a woman presses a hidden alarm bell whilst they're all up there. Down the stairs they come and a milkman tries to hold the door against them from outside. Joey shoots at him through the glass and takes most of his head off. He's still doing life and Frank and Bernie Beattie, who was the driver, got fifteen years apiece. But what a bit of luck for Jackie sitting in the nick with a cast iron genuine alibi.

Bernie Beattie was unlucky on that raid. When he's got the car going he comes to a crossroads and near enough hits another car. The driver's a woman and she says she's had a good look at him and can pick him out on a parade, so when he's nicked he goes on one at

Wood Green police station. He had my old brief Jimmy Fellowes defending and organising the parade and they stand outside in the cold for the better part of fifty minutes whilst she goes up and down the line trying to make her mind up between Bernie and a couple of the others on the parade. Eventually she picks out poor Bernie. The jury wore it. That was all there was against him. That, and knowing the others. Nowadays I don't suppose on that sort of ID the prosecution would even charge him.

I was in the nick a lot with Frank. He was a good man. Never give way. He'd stand side by side with you. There's a story about him that he had one of those inflatable life-size Japanese rubber dolls smuggled into him whilst he was in the nick, and being the good man he was he let it out to his mates. Of course, eventually the screws had to find it and they confiscated it. I expect they used it themselves.

12 June 1975

Probably June hasn't been a lucky month for me and court cases. This was the day my family went to Court to try and get me represented before the Visiting Magistrates in Bristol Prison on a bit of violence against screws. They had that lawyer Stephen Sedley – he's come a long way since then and now he's a Lord Justice of Appeal – who was very keen on civil rights representing me, and they were trying to get an injunction to stop the case against me until I could have a brief.

First of all Eva got hold of the civil rights solicitors Bindmans and they sent a telegram to the governor asking that nothing happen until they could see me and get my side of the story. Of course that met with a blank, so they spoke to the clerk of the Board of Visitors and he said he wouldn't advise the board to let me have a brief nor to adjourn, so the solicitors issued a writ against the board to try and get them banned from hearing the case.

It came up in front of that Lord Denning who was meant to be such a great champion of the people himself, but he wasn't a champion of prisoners' rights. He was the one who said it was better if the people accused of the Birmingham Bombing stayed in prison the rest of their lives rather than it seem as if a British copper had faked the evidence against them. My family sent me the judgement in my case and Denning had gone on and on about how if you were in the armed forces and you were on a disciplinary charge you were brought up in front of your commanding officer and he dealt with you there and then and you didn't have any representation. If people were allowed briefs then there would be delays. All that was needed to be fair was that I should know what charge I was on and let me present my case. Another of the judges said that there was plenty of times when there was no need for representation for justice to be done and seen to be done. There wasn't much seeing. It was all in a closed room with no one watching what happened.

Of course what the judges said was a lot of rubbish. There was no way I could present my case properly. Nor could any other prisoner. In those days if a screw said Black was White they'd all nod and say of course it is. Denning ended up saying that the court shouldn't establish a precedent by letting me be represented.

Nearly ten years later I tried again. Stephen Sedley was my brief this time as well and we didn't get any more change than he had the last time. By this time it was 1984 and I'd lost something like seven years' remission. Without that I'd have been out, so what we tried to do was to get the decisions of the Boards of Visitors going back as far as Leicester in January 1968 quashed because I wasn't represented. By now a bloke called Tarrant had sued the Home Office and he'd made a bit of progress. He'd got a ruling that although the Board of Visitors didn't have to allow a prisoner to be legally represented, they could do so or they could let you have a friend or adviser with you if you asked.

Of course the court got round it saying there had been too long a delay. The Leicester case was sixteen years ago and the latest was two and a half, but what it amounted to was that I'd got the equivalent of eighteen years without any representation. They also said that no one could remember properly what happened on the applications and whether I had actually asked to be represented, so that it was prejudicial to the administration of justice. They said that I was far too late. I don't know about prejudicial to the administration of justice, but it was prejudicial to me.

17 June 1950

It's always a bit frightening when you're left behind on a raid but really it's part and parcel of the job. You've got to be prepared for it. It's more adrenaline than actual fright. If it's fright you shouldn't be doing it. But there's the worry you're going to be left behind. I've been left once. It was in 1950, which was generally a good time for me. We'd gone on one in Holborn. That's me and Jimmy Ford, the ex-boxer, Dido Frett and Albert Baffy driving. We were just doing a wages snatch; money going to a night safe, simple thing altogether. The driver didn't move from the wheel whatever happened. Jimmy, he would be like me on the pavement. I'd have my cosh and be steaming into the people who were carrying the bags and it would be Dido's job to get them. Jimmy's job was to watch my back, make sure no one got up behind me.

Wages snatches was fairly rare. You could count on your hand the number of firms in London who was doing them. In fact for a time we was the only one. People would have loved to have joined us when we was the Friday Gang. They brought things to us.

This time, however, there was a couple of rugby playing types who decided to have a go; they come out of nowhere. We were on our way back to the motor and

Jimmy and Dido got in but these people grabbed me. I fought like a tiger, give them a few blows with my cosh as they steamed into me, and I managed to wriggle away. Then I was on my toes with them after me. Once I was round the back of Holborn in them little alleyways and things, I was all right for I knew them quite well. I got myself down to the Cross and got the underground back to South London for the divvi up.

The only time I think I've really been frightened was when that Governor Lawton tried to do me in Pentonville. I'd caused him a lot of aggro and he'd had me put in a straitjacket on a soft mattress. I couldn't turn over properly and I was suffocating. He come to my cell and I remember him saying, 'It won't be long, now' and that give me strength to keep going. That's why I strung him and his dog both up on Wandsworth Common when I got the chance.

I was never frightened in a fight and I've had some good ones in my time. If you was frightened you was beat from the start. The other man could see it in your eyes. The best straightener I've ever had ran three days and it was in Portland Borstal with a boy called Wilson. He was a bit bigger than me and he came from the mines outside Leeds. He kept on niggling me, saying things about Cockney bastards. The screws would turn blind eyes to fights then, provided they were just fist fights and no one was trying to put the boot in. 'It made for good order', they said. 'Get it out of the boys' system' that sort of thing. We fought three consecutive days. Our faces were out to here and eventually the screws said it was enough and we were to shake hands. No one won but we didn't half have a good go. I never saw him after that. He wasn't a thief. I think he was in for some sort of assault; he'd had a fight in a pub.

Right My sister Eva
and her husband
Jimmy Brindle.

Below Me as
captain of St
Patrick's Football
Team (1935–6).
I'm holding the ball.

ST. PATRICK'S
FOOTBALL
TEAM
1935–6

Above I can still take a good punch. I'm with a Gangland Tour party (the tour I conduct around London's East End). We had stopped off at the Repton A.B.C

Left I used to take telephone bookings for the Gangland Tour. Now a lot of i is done on the Internet.

Left Marilyn took this of me, Charlie Richardson, Lenny McLean and the promoter Alex Steene. Funnily enough we were at dinner at the Law Society in Chancer Lane.

Above Me and Marilyn having a quiet drink in The British Lion.

Below My youngest son Francis who played for Brighton & Hove Albion, until he was injured.

© Bushell-Adams

Left Mickey Rourke, me and Gary Stretch – the model and boxer. Even though I don't need bodyguards they make a fine pair.

Right I can still put the frighteners on when I have to.

Below left I often go to dinner shows and sometimes Tommy, Marilyn's Dad, comes with me

Below right Charlie Kray, Roy Shaw, me and Dave Clarke – who was a great campaigner for the release of Reggie.

Ron Gray & Scott Murray

CHASE SPORTING CLUB

Presents...

A Gentlemens Evening With

'MAD' FRANKIE FRASER

FORMER EAST END GANGSTER WITH THE
RICHARDSON'S & THE KRAY TWINS

PLUS

TOMMY WHISBY
THE GREAT TRAIN ROBBER

Comedian Ronnie Stewart & Master of Ceremonies Barry DeLacy

THURSDAY 24TH JUNE '99

Starts at 7.30pm

Bar Spot
Sports Bar & Grill

85 High Green, Cannock, Staffs. Tel: 01543 573131

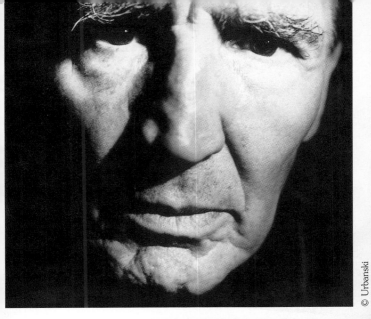

© Urbanski

Right I'm in a familiar role in this publicity still for an album called *Return of the Mekon*.

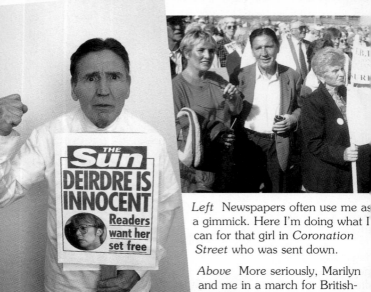

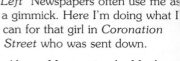

Left Newspapers often use me as a gimmick. Here I'm doing what I can for that girl in *Coronation Street* who was sent down.

Above More seriously, Marilyn and me in a march for British-Italian pensioners in Clerkenwell

Above Mike Dalton, the boxing promoter, often has me up speaking at the dinner and charity shows he runs apart from boxing.

Right Billy Hill.

Below left Ronnie's grave.

Below right This is me and Danny just after he found my gold chain.

LEGEND

RONALD KRAY

BORN   DIED
4TH OCTOBER 1933.   17TH MARCH 1995.

NEVER TO BE FORGOTTEN

Left Me and Marilyn in the dressing room before we did our show in Jermyn Street, Piccadilly.

Left With Marilyn at Barbara Windsor's 60th Birthday bash.

Below A surprise photo – on a sad day.

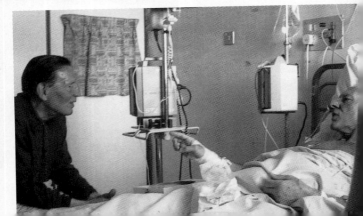

24 June 1998

I did an interview for the *Independent* today. People wrote in asking me questions about how to get bloodstains out of woolly jumpers (I said ask Scotland Yard) and did I dye my hair (yes). But no one asked me what I thought of drugs.

Although people have put my name up on several occasions I've never been the King of Drugs in South London or anywhere else for that matter. Joe Wilkins, who I'd done a lot of work with over the years, stuck my name up when he was in trouble over a load of drugs. Said he was frightened of me and the court wore it.

Then there was the trouble at Turnmills when I was shot. In fact it was the *Independent* said I'd fallen foul of the Adams family in a drug deal, but that was a load of cobblers. The last time people put my name up was when my boy David got involved with the crooked copper John Donald who got twelve years. The Pros said I was a mastermind. If I was a mastermind I wouldn't be living in a rented flat off the Walworth Road, that's for certain.

In fairness I'm asked time and again to go into drugs and often it's difficult to turn it down. Even for a small investment you can make a hundred grand easy. It all depends on how good your information is and how good the people are who's supplying you. And that's where the trouble starts. In the days when I was working you knew each other. They came from the next house or block of flats or you'd been at school with them. They had a background and there'd be two or three or four of you. If someone was a wrong 'un everyone in the neighbourhood knew and you stayed shy of him.

Then in the 1950s came the great escapes by the spy George Blake and Frank Mitchell and the government set up an inquiry under that Lord Mountbatten before the IRA blew him up. He recommended that villains should be dispersed around the country instead of being near their homes and together with their friends in the nick. The result was that we all learned a lot more about other areas and what jobs might come on offer in them. But it also meant that we had to rely more on people we didn't know. Prison friendships aren't friendships you make as a child, and it's much more difficult checking out the credentials of someone, say, in Manchester. Of course it can be done. I could always get in touch with Bobby McDonald, the barrow king there, and ask if he knew someone and could vouch for them and in Glasgow with Arthur Thompson there would be no problem, but overall it made it that much more difficult. You couldn't expect Bobby to know exactly what the score was in Liverpool. It's the same with drugs. You're relying on people you don't know and in any deal there's always a number who can go hooky on you.

In the old days once you'd done the job the money was cut up and that was the end. Now with drugs it's not like that. Say, you've got fifty grand to put in a deal, you can make that into a good half million if you're lucky but you need that luck. There may be up to twenty people involved at any one time and every one of them is potentially a loose link.

So now I've got fifty grand and I've got to go to someone. That person would have to get the drugs and although he'll say he has them, the chances are that he's got to go to someone for them himself – there's so many middlemen. Then there's the chance you'll be ripped off completely or that, through no real fault of the man you've got to first, the gear'll be duff or at least not top quality. There's so many parcels floating about. Which is genuine?

Then someone's actually got to get the gear. There's always the possibility that the police or Customs will grab it legitimately or that the man'll do a deal with them – or even, like poor Charlie Kray found when he started boasting, that the men you are talking to are undercover coppers.

Then you've got to get a lorry or at least a camper if you're bringing in puff. If it's Charlie it's not so bulky to move. Then when you've got it yourself you've got to sell it. And are you sure the buyer's straight? Will he grass on you or turn you over for your dough? There's so much of that going about you wouldn't believe it. Why do you think there are all these killings? Drug deals gone wrong, that's what a lot are about.

It's not like finding a job and doing it yourself. The most successful thief is the one who works by himself and doesn't have to rely on anyone else. And the next successful thief is where you're working with just one of the family. I know people who have come a cropper with their own family, but overall that's the safest combination.

Drugs isn't like that. There's just too many in the chain. And the next thing is there's people in the game who aren't real criminals. When they get caught they'll roll over and name names to save their own skin. I just don't think it's worth it. And anyway, like I say, I don't have fifty grand.

Am I sorry my boys have gone into drugs? I can't rightly say I am. That's the culture now for all walks of life and they're just supplying a need.

30 June 1930

This was the day my old friend Ruby Sparkes, well he was young Ruby then, made a break for it from Wandsworth. Him and Jim Turner had only been sent down at the Old Bailey in the May when they got five years each for motor car robberies and they didn't hang around. What they did was communicate with each other in their cells by putting cups to the wall so they could hear what was being said. They'd also put saucers of water on the floor so when the warders came tramping down the corridor in their heavy boots the water would ripple and they'd know someone was about.

Security wasn't what it is now, and off the exercise yard there was a path which led through the prison doctor's garden to the outside. All they had to do was get over an inner wall. There was two screws watching the morning exercise and one seeing to the men who were in the lavatory when they made a run for it. Some warder threw his truncheon at Ruby, hitting him between the shoulders and knocking him back off the wall. Jim kept on climbing and was away. That was when the screws really laid into Ruby. He was so covered in blood the Chief Officer couldn't tell whether it was him or Jim and when he was asked Ruby did the right thing and give the name Turner.

Of course it wasn't simply a spur-of-the-moment job. What it was really was to get Ruby out, and his girlfriend Lilian, the bobbed-haired bandit, was the organiser. Now she was a class girl. Came from a Jewish family in the East End. She'd be in her late twenties at the time. She tried to get Ruby out of Manchester a few years earlier. This time she organised three cars, one waiting outside, the second she'd hired and drove herself and the third waiting just outside Barnet. She was a tidy girl. She'd returned the second car to the company before anyone suspected anything. The papers was full of how it was a young man in a felt hat and new kid gloves drove the first car. The coppers all knew it was her behind it but they were never able to prove it. She'd hired a car for the day. So what? She was a good girl. It must have been a great disappointment to her when it wasn't Ruby who showed up but she stuck to it.

Through Ruby, when I was older I got to know her quite a bit.

Poor old Jim didn't last long on the outside. The police lost the trail in Barnet and there were suggestions he'd get away to the Continent with a forged passport, but in fact he only lasted three more days. Someone opened their mouth on a bus and a passenger overheard and went to the police. They found Jim in a house in Rye Hill Park in Peckham and went in mob handed whilst he was sitting in an upstairs room, smoking a pipe and reading the evening paper. Nevertheless he still had a go for it. He leaped out of the window and went flying thirty feet into the garden but he was injured in the fall and that was that.

Jim was a classy thief. Years later I met him in Wandsworth. He'd got the top job then. He was in the woodshed, cutting logs for the boilers and the screws' fires.

2 July 1999

Mr Justice Lawton's father wasn't the only man I tried to hang. Me and Jimmy Robson did a man in the grounds of a club in Lewisham during the war. It's Jimmy's birthday today. He was 82 this year and he's in a care home where I sometimes go and see him.

There used to be only three real drinkers in South London during the war. There were others, of course, but these were the big ones. To get a licence you had to be 100 per cent. They were all legal but you only got the chaps in. Market traders, you called them coster-mongers in those days, street bookmakers, thieves, they were the only ones who could afford to get in. The ordinary man and woman hadn't the money. The authorities were very strict about people spending their money. If anyone got done for illegal gambling then apart from a fine from the beak or, if they were running the show, a bit of bird, they all got a lecture about how they should be putting their money into National Savings instead of wasting it. You never got brasses in them; shoplifters who were game girls, yes, but not brasses.

As I recall the clubs were the Bungalow at Streatham, the '21' on Clapham Common and this one at Lewisham. We called it the Lewisham Club but I don't know if that was its proper name. It was a big house set in its own grounds with lots of trees and a driveway with a bend in it. It was a bit like the houses in one of those black and white Boris Karloff films you get on the telly nowadays. You half thought Bela Lugosi would be waiting up the drive.

Anyway it was just before Christmas and Jimmy and me was in there. You half knew everyone, there were never strangers. If someone new came in it was if he was vouched for by someone. That day there was this man who wasn't right. Jimmy and me thought he was an undercover copper, sort of watching so the club could be done for illegal drinking. We got him in conversation and he still didn't seem right. He didn't know anyone and he kept looking shifty, so when he went out to the lavatory Jim and I just got hold of him, found a bit of rope – there was always useful things laying around in that club – and took him out and strung him up on one of the trees in the drive. It was starting to snow at the time and I remember we just left him there. There were people coming and going all the time so I don't suppose he stayed up there very long but it was a warning. 'You've been ID'd. Don't come back'. And as far as I know he never did.

Poor Jim's been very ill recently; been in hospital most of this last winter.

8 July 1965

Ronnie Biggs escaped today. He'd only been in less than two years and they never got him again. He got out over the wall at Wandsworth, leaving a mailbag behind which he'd been sewing and which he'd been paid for. The screw used to say he owed him for it. In fact he was the second of the robbers to escape – Charlie Wilson had got out of Winson Green the year before – but Ronnie's stayed out the longest ever out of an English nick. It's a record I don't suppose will be broken. Before him it was the catman Ray Jones, who broke his legs when he got out of Pentonville and stayed out around eighteen months before someone shopped him.

In a way once Charlie got out all the others paid for it. Ronnie had to leave his clothing outside, had to have his light on in his cell all night. He was checked and they moved him and the others around regularly. He only got an hour's exercise and two hours' work a day and Ronnie used to have to sit in the front row of the mailbag shop. He wrote to his MP, asking if he could help get the conditions relaxed, but he never got a reply. He'd wanted to do his bird the easy way but they weren't going to let him and so he decided he'd have to escape.

He got a message to the team who'd sprung Charlie Wilson but they thought there was too much heat about, and he spoke to Paul Seabourne who was doing a four and who'd organised a mass break-out a few years earlier. There was talk of a helicopter and a commando raid on the prison but Ronnie didn't want no blood spilled on his account. It had to be one of them escapes which was a matter of timing. There was no point in someone chucking a ladder over the wall and hoping Ronnie saw it. So what they come up with was a furniture van with part of the roof cut out and a platform built inside. The idea was to drive the lorry up to the prison wall and then haul the platform up so it was level with the top. Ronnie's wife put up ten grand for Paul after his release.

Ronnie got out during exercise and it nearly got messed up through no fault of Ronnie's or the others who'd organised it except they were so good-hearted. He'd been lucky that an old mate, Eric Flowers, was on remand and could get messages through on visits – the screws were sitting in on his own – and they fixed the day for 8 July. Charmain took their kids to the zoo and got a parking ticket for her car so she had an alibi and Ronnie and Eric went out on exercise at half two. Two other cons had been given the promise of £500 each to help block the screws and half an hour later two ladders came down the wall and up went Ronnie and Eric. The trouble was so did Andy Anderson, who was with me in the Parkhurst riot, and another bloke. They didn't know what to do with them and so they let them off in South London and gave them a few quid each. Andy made his way to Tottenham Court Road and Atlantic Machines, where we had a whip round and Stanley Baker, the actor, gave him some clothes. Then he hid out with Eva for a bit before I arranged with Arthur Thomson, the big man in Glasgow, to have him up there.

From then on for Ronnie it was just one move after another. Him and Eric stayed in Bermondsey that night, drinking champagne and watching their escape on the box. Then he went down to Bognor and stayed on the South Coast for a time. Part of his money went on plastic surgery and three months later him and Eric were shipped out to Amsterdam and then back to Paris.

I'm never sure that plastic surgery is all it's cracked up to be; at any rate not when it's being done to change appearances. By all accounts John Dillinger nearly died when he had plastic surgery and there was a guy in Mexico recently died under the anaesthetic when they was altering his appearance. Both times the doctors died a few months later.[1] But that didn't happen with Ronnie although he used to say it was agony. Then he split up with Eric and they went separately to Sydney. He was nearly broke by now and was working as a carpenter in a television studios when the police got a tip off and picked up Eric at the flat he was sharing with Ronnie and Charmain. She was nicked but Ronnie was gone. There was one good thing; she got $65,000 from a newspaper. With some of the money he got a new passport and went to Rio. It all went well there for a while until some reporter found out who he was and did a deal for Ronnie to tell his story. Bad luck for him the man's editor had told the police and who's at the door but the copper, Jack Slipper.

Fortunately for Ronnie he'd got his Brazilian girl-friend in the club and under their law you couldn't deport the father of a Brazilian child, so he was allowed to stay. He's remained close to the boy, Michael. In 1977 some mercenaries had a go at kidnapping him but he survived it. He got kidnapped again in 1981 and taken to Barbados before he was eventually released and

---

[1] The drug baron Amado Carrillo Fuentes died in a Mexico City clinic in 1997. The body of Jaime Godoy Singh, who led the team of surgeons, was found in an oil drum on the Mexico City–Acapulco highway. In fact Dillinger's doctor survived. It was the doctor who botched the plastic surgery on Alvin Karpis the Public Enemy No. 1 and Fred Barker, one of the 'Ma' Barker family, who died.

returned to Rio. Then there was a film and he wrote a book and helped with a novel. Then the government here tried to get him extradited and they got a knock-back.

For a time it was all wine, women and song but the wine's dried up and the last few years haven't been good to him. As the years went by things got worse for Ronnie. The flat he lived in overlooks the city but there's a lot of street crime and he doesn't have much money. He'd made a bit of money out of being a tourist attraction. For 25 quid he'd tell his story and give you a meal and you could buy a T-shirt or have your photo taken with him. When Marilyn went out to see him she'd just sold her flat and she bunged him six hundred quid.

At the back end of 1999 Ronnie had a series of strokes and the last I heard he was in a wheelchair and wasn't really able to speak; the only way he could talk, so to speak, was to wave his hands. People say he should have a pardon and be allowed to come home and die and I agree, but I don't think there's a chance with this government and its tough-on-crime policy. It would be a sign of weakness. He's made a monkey out of them all these years and they'll want their pound of flesh. After all, it's not a question of his never having been been found guilty and his going back to court and maybe getting a sympathetic judge who'd give him a light. He'd just go straight into the nick again and hope for parole or a pardon and he might win the lottery before he got that. I think if it had been me and I'd been in his position I'd have come home years ago. I know I'd have had to do say a ten, but then I'd have been out and about. Every year it must have been harder for him.

This was another big day for crime because it was the one that really did for the Scotsman Paddy Meehan. The Scots boys used to come down here and do a lot of work and Paddy was one of them. Sometimes it was contract, as with a safe, and sometimes it was just to get away from the slops, as they called them in Glasgow. It was the same with us. If things got a bit warm you could always go to Arthur Thompson and he'd find you a bit of work to keep you out of the way. It was the same when I went on the run over Harry Rogers. Albert Dimes fixed it up with One-Armed Lou in Soho that I should go to Paris. I had a right good time there but I did a bit of work to earn my keep. Nothing very heavy. I couldn't say 'This is a stick-up' in French so it was a question of going to help lean on a few people.

Paddy Meehan was a good safebreaker but he was an unlucky thief. One you wouldn't really want to work with. Not that he wasn't game; game as they come. It was just he didn't have luck and that's what you want in a man.

One of the first times he's down here is after there's been a real ruckus up in Glasgow and Arthur Thompson's gone and stabbed Teddy Miller in a row over dough which is needed to screw a bank in Old Street down here. Teddy's fit enough to work a couple of days later but Arthur's not going to work with him, so Paddy and Miller get a third guy. It's a disaster, almost a ready-eye. Teddy Miller and the third guy get nicked on the job and Paddy gets away. But the next job he's on down here, a safe in a Co-op in Edmonton with Billy Gentry, he gets a pull. He always reckoned a bird had grassed them. If he was right Billy didn't have much luck with birds either, because years later that model Tina Meer grassed him and a whole load of others, and Billy got a lot of bird over that.

But Paddy's real troubles came when an old girl in Ayr died in 1968 after a tie-up. Paddy and James Griffiths – who was the only man to get off the Isle of Wight – were in the frame because the robbers had been heard calling themselves Pat and Jim. The whole thing was dodgy. Paddy got picked out on a voice parade when he was the only one who spoke. It was also accepted by Meehan that he and Griffiths had been in the area. The old girl's husband also ID'd him. Paddy agreed he'd been in Ayr and anyway two girls him and Griffiths and Meehan had given a lift to also picked him out. There wasn't no question of an ID for Jim. He'd been killed in a blazing shoot-out with the coppers.

You can have an 8–7 majority verdict in Scotland where you've got 15 jurors, and a majority found Paddy guilty and he got life. There was all sorts of rumours flying around and Joe Beltrami, the well-known brief up there, was doing all he could to get Paddy released. It was now rumoured that two other guys, Ian Waddell and Tank McGuiness, were the actual robbers.

A few years later Tank got beaten unconscious close to the Celtic football ground and died in the Royal Infirmary. Although it was never proved, it was put about he'd been done over his involvement in the Ross murder. According to Joe Beltrami he'd started dropping by the office and giving out hints over the case. Once Tank was dead Beltrami thought he could now tell what Tank had been saying and established that Waddell's alibi was false for the murder. Shortly after the killing he'd come into a lot of dough although he was unemployed at the time. Paddy was pardoned in May 1976 and they did Ian Waddell for the murder. After an hour he got chucked. It makes you think when there's these juries out for days and weeks nowadays. A few years later it was his turn to get done. Paddy got quite a bit of dough in compensation. He was never really as pleased with Joe Beltrami as he should have been and he brought out a book blaming him for his getting convicted in the first place. I heard he'd died a few years back of throat cancer. Those Scots are big smokers. There was an inquiry into the case and it come up with the theory that all four of them were on it and that's how Tank got a conscience and the old girl's husband

heard the names Pat and Jim. Shows you should keep
your mouth shut on a raid.

15 July 1951

It's nearly fifty years since Straffen was sentenced for killing a little girl. I knew him in Broadmoor and then again when I was in Wandsworth. He was mental then and he'd got to be even worse. I don't know how he's survived.

It was 15 July that he did the little girl Brenda Goddard in Bath. She was out in the garden and when she was called in to get ready for Sunday School the foster parents discovered she was missing. The police found her body that evening in a wood. She'd been assaulted but at least she hadn't been raped.

Straffen had only come out of the local bin in Bristol six months earlier. He'd been in care in a school for mentally defective kids when he was ten and when he was seventeen he assaulted a kid saying 'What would you do if I killed you? I've done it before'. I don't think there was any evidence he had, though. That's what got him committed to a bin.

There was a description of a man wearing a suit similar to the one Straffen had been given when they let him out. Remember, in those days people didn't travel far and nutters were known in the community so it wasn't that difficult to trace him. But once they found him he denied it, and since there was no evidence they

had to let him go. The next girl he did was Cicely
Batstone who was going to a kid's matinee at the cinema
in Bath. This time there was some identification and a
couple said they'd seen Straffen with her. He coughed
it straight away. Said something like 'It didn't take long'.
At the assizes he was found unfit to plead and they sent
him to Broadmoor.

He wasn't long in Broadmoor before he escaped in
1952. He was out four hours and by the time they found
him another little girl, Linda Bowyer, had been killed.
According to the coppers the first thing he said was 'I
didn't kill the little girl' and the one in charge replied
'No one's suggested anyone's been killed'. That's what
did for him. They weren't just going to put him back in
a hospital. It was a proper trial. Funnily, although he'd
been a nutter all his life and was until the day of the
killing, by this time he wasn't a nutter. He was fit to
stand trial and they sentenced him to a topping. He got
reprieved but there was no mental hospital for him this
time. It was straight in the nick.

I'd had no truck with him in Broadmoor. Tall,
angular, dopey-looking, he wasn't the full ticket. In fact
I barely knew who he was but everyone knew him in
Wandsworth.

He did his bird the hard way. In those days he was on
E wing and grub would be brought to your cell. Some of
the screws really topped him up. There was no canteen
as there is now and the food came in tins, one over the
other. There'd be a potato or a bit of corned beef in the
top one and soup, if you could call it that, in the bottom
one. Once a month you might get tinned apricots.
They'd walk past his cell without giving him anything
to eat and sometimes they'd open his door and then
walk on past. It was a favourite trick. By this time he
was terrified. He'd had so many knockings about. If he
was brought out to work he'd be back in his cell within
a few hours because he'd had a clumping. If he rang his

bell it would be ignored. Some screws would give prisoners the odd cigarette to give him a bashing. I don't think he even knew how to complain and if he did know he was too frightened to do it.

Of course no one at governor or deputy governor level ever got to hear of this. You couldn't apply to be segregated. The only way you weren't in the main prison was if you was on some disciplinary offence. In fact it was for the likes of Straffen that Rule 43 came out.

Funnily I was never in the same prison as him again. He'll be about seventy I should think and he must be completely mad. They'll never let him out.[1]

---

[1] John Thomas Straffen was originally convicted at Taunton Assizes. He escaped from Broadmoor on 29 April 1952 and was recaptured a little over four hours later. He was reprieved on 29 August 1952.

28 July 1998

I read in the papers that Donald Hume was dead. I first met him in Dartmoor in 1957. He'd been found in a wood down in Gloucestershire half-decomposed and they'd had to identify him from his teeth. I'd known him both in prison, when he was serving time for Setty, and after he came out of prison from Switzerland the second time. He was one of the few people who get convicted of murder and then come out and do it again. I can't think of too many, not in this country anyway.

There was certainly Jimmy Essex but both his got knocked down to manslaughter, and there was that Donald Chesney in Scotland but he got chucked on the first, the one where he did his mother. Joey Martin I suppose you could put in that category, but he got his first knocked down to manslaughter as well. Killed a brass at a party playing Russian Roulette and hadn't been out six months when he was on a wages snatch which went wrong in Wood Green in 1965. He got convicted for killing a milkman who tried to hold the door closed against him and the others to stop them getting out. Joe was like a lion in prison. He wouldn't stand no nonsense. He tried to get out when John McVicar broke out of Durham. Joey got life. He must have done nearly thirty-five. I think it wasn't for the shooting of the milkman but it was an accumulation. Like they thought he got away with the first so they're having their revenge. I believe he's out now but at the very worst, one good thing is that at last he's been moved down the categories and so if he's got any luck at all he should be having day release soon.

But getting back to Donald Hume. Duncan Webb, the reporter, married his wife whilst he was away and he was terrified that Donald would get released and come after him. Webb was a bit of a funny devil. Don's wife was a night club hostess and I think he had a bit of a thing for brasses altogether. He was very hot at supressing vice. He had a column in the *People* and he was really one of their top men. You know the headlines 'I name Hull vice capital of Europe', that sort of thing. He had it in for the Messinas and the other Maltese who were really the vice kings of London in the fifties and sixties. When someone got convicted after one of his exposures he would put an advertisement on the front page of *The Times* 'Thanks to St Jude'. Billy Hill and me and the others used to take the piss out of him in Peter Mario's in Gerrard Street – it's now a Chinese called Harbour City – saying we expected Don to be released any day soon.

Don was involved in one of the really big murder cases of 1949, or any other year for that matter. Stanley Setty, who was an Arab and whose real name was Sulman Seti, was a second-hand car dealer, money lender, bit of a receiver, that sort of thing in Warren Street. His brother Max was much more up-market and he ran a night club, the Blue Angel in Berkeley Street, Mayfair, which was really fashionable with the young set, no brasses or over-priced drinks or things like that.

On 5 October 1949 the body of Stanley Setty was dumped from an aeroplane into the Essex marshes. Known as a banker for the black market and born in Baghdad, he ran his business from the pavement

around Warren Street, then home to the London second-hand car trade and all sorts of dishonest dealing.

The day before, Stanley had drawn £1,005 from his
bank to pay for a car. And on the next day Donald hired
an Auster from the United Flying Services Club at
Elstree, flew over the Essex coast and dropped two
parcels. He landed at Southend aerodrome and rented a
car to bring him back to his flat in Golders Green. The
next day he returned to Southend from where he flew
the plane over Gravesend and dumped another parcel
wrapped in felt and tied with twine. A fortnight later
one of the parcels was brought in by the tide at
Tillingham on the Essex marshes and in it was a bit of
Stanley.

Actually quite a bit, because it was all there except
the head and legs. Stanley had been stabbed quite a few
times and then had his head cut off. They found out
who it was through his fingerprints. He'd done a bit of
bird for fraud.

It was quite easy to trace Hume through the flying.
After all, he'd rented the plane in his own name. He'd
just miscalculated when he dropped the parcels. He
thought the parcels had been dropped far enough out to
sea and he was wrong.

He came up with a story about how he had agreed
with two men, 'Mac' and Green, to pilot an aeroplane
for them on a smuggling trip for a fifty quid fee. On 5
October they had called at his home with parcels
containing what they said were 'hot' plates used for
forging clothing coupons and they wanted them dropped. After the first flight on his return to Golders Green
he found them, along with a third man called 'Boy',
waiting outside his flat and he agreed to drop the third
parcel for another £100.

Of course no one found Mac or Boy or Green and
Donald was charged with murder. The judge was took
ill in the first trial, and they had to start all over again.

The evidence was strong against him. The Pros maintained that Setty had been killed in Hume's flat and that was where he'd cut him up. They had the notes which Setty had got out of the bank. Then someone identified a knife as being one which Don had asked him to sharpen. He had taken a carpet to be cleaned and that come up in evidence as well. What he had going for him was there wasn't a single fingerprint of Setty's in Hume's flat, nor had any neighbour heard suspicious noises on the night of 4 October or the next morning. He also called Dr Camps, the pathologist, who said that someone must have heard him sawing poor old Setty. It was enough to get the jury to disagree.

Just when it looked like there was going to be a second trial the Pros offered a deal. Don should plead to being an accessory after the fact. I know Don was confident he'd just get a few years but they loaded twelve on him.

I knew him in the nick. You'd pass him by without noticing him. He was pleasant enough, very likeable really, but there again he'd got a spiteful turn. Once when he was playing table tennis he was losing and he deliberately stood on the ball and not only ruined the game but it meant we couldn't play until we'd saved up and got another.

He got out in 1958 and immediately sold his story, 'I killed Setty . . . and got away with murder', to the *Sunday Pictorial*. I think he got two grand for the story. He had, he said, stabbed Setty with a knife in a quarrel but he never made it clear what the quarrel was about. He'd told me it was because Setty had done him for some dough over a car. He might have stood for a beating but he was funny about money. He told me he'd done another two people as well. After that he changed his name and that year he went and shot a bank cashier in August and another in November. Both of them survived and there was no charges.

Then in January the next year he did another bank, this time in Zurich, and when a taxi-driver tried to stop him he killed him. Now he got to life, after which the president of the court declared 'Life imprisonment for this kind of man means for life. He will never be let out of jail – not this one'.

But of course he was. He was sent back to England and went to Broadmoor which is where he met Ronnie who told him to get in touch with me when he got out, saying he'd get a bit of help from me. He tracked me down through Marilyn's flower stall and we met in the Waldorf hotel in Aldwych. Marilyn and me were still living at the Angel at the time and he came and did some electrical work, putting some lights in the garage at the back of the flat. I held him by his legs as he leaned out the window.

He was still game. He said if I found anything he would want to come along on it. I saw him a few times but then he drifted away. I suppose his mental troubles must have overtook him again.

28 July 1999

This was when Lennie McLean died. I never really knew him much before he became famous and I never saw him fight except for video clips, particularly that famous one where Gipsy Bradshaw tries to nut him before the bell for the first round and Lennie just does him, punching, butting, kicking. No need for a points decision there. It can't have lasted half a minute from the moment the referee called them together. In fact I never really heard of Lennie before I met him. In his book he says he was related to Bobby Warren, who wasn't with me on the Spot slashing but still got done for it. But Bobby had never mentioned him to me.

Funnily I was never with Lennie in the nick. The first time I met him was at the Law Society's Hall in Chancery Lane, which is a funny place for the pair of us to be, but what it was was a benefit for a boxing timekeeper who'd had a stroke or something. Me and Charlie Richardson met him there. At the time he was minding a club in Beak Street and when Marilyn wanted to record a song he recommended Jack Adams, who was Georgie Cornell's nephew and who had a recording studio.

He gives me a good gee in his book but I think he's got it wrong. Not that it's not welcome. He says that just after me and Bobby Warren got the sevens over Spot I went up to the biggest screw in Wandsworth, give him a prod and say 'Behave yourself'. I know they call me mad but I'm not that mad. Anyway I was only there two days before I was transferred to Bristol. Still, it's a good story.

The story I like best about him is when he's got eighteen months for manslaughter after he killed a nutter who was exposing himself on the stage of the Hippodrome and he died when Lenny pulled him off. Lennie's in his cell and a young kid's put in with him. Lennie tells him there's to be no farting because there's nothing worse than having someone in your cell who's breaking wind the whole time. The kid nods because he's terrified. The next thing Lennie blows two great big ones and says to the boy 'They're for both of us'.

Once I'd met him we used to see each other a bit and Marilyn and I went to Pinewood where she was going to sing the song over the credits for his film but, sadly, it never came to anything. He was terrific in that *Lock, Stock and Two Smoking Barrels*. I hope if I do another film I'll be as good.

30 July 1948

This was the day when Jack Spot's luck started to turn against him. I never liked him. I never liked the way he cut people, but when they cut him he'd Pros them. But to give him credit he had some good people like George and Jimmy Wood working for him so he can't have been bad all the time.

I've never actually been able to make up my mind just how big Spot was in the London Airport robbery, but so many people say he was the organiser, much as it goes against me to admit it I suppose he must have been. It was a brilliant operation but it was one which went wrong because of a grass.

Heathrow Airport was called London then. It had replaced Croydon, which Bert Marsh done, as the big airport and word was there was a bonded warehouse with £388,000 worth of diamonds in and a further £250,000 to come in. The idea was to get in and dope the coffee of the warehouse staff but someone went hooky and talked to the security. So instead of there being doped warehouse staff, there was alive and well Flying Squad coppers waiting for them. It was meant to be a triumph of the Ghost Squad. There was a terrific fight and Billy Benstead and Franny Daniels got away and so did Teddy Machin, but the others were nicked.

George Wood got an eight and Jimmy another one on top.

The story is that there'd been a tie-up by a fellow, Jack Stanley, from South London, and some others. One geezer who should have been in on it, but wasn't, thought he should still have his share. They'd burned a safe and the take had come to around 57 grand. They wouldn't give this geezer his cut and many people think he was the one who lollied the airport job. Poor old Jack was heavy into tie-ups and extortion. He died the year of the job. Killed in a car crash.

I hadn't seen George Wood in years and I ran into him in the Prince Alice over at Forest Gate in May last year. I'd gone over there to do a thing for a television company. He was looking a bit frail, but then he's older than me, but he was looking just as dapper as he always did. Him and his brother, Jimmy, were big men when they were young; men you should look up to.

There's not a lot of them left from that robbery. Jimmy's been dead some time and sadly George died a few months ago. So is Teddy Machin who got shot in a domestic over in East Ham. I used to think Jock McQuillan was on it but I've been told he wasn't. Then there was poor old Alfie Roome who, after he come out, swallowed poison on the pavement outside the Ford plant at Dagenham. He'd thought his old woman was having an affair with a paper stall owner where she'd been working, and he tried to do them both before he topped himself. He'd gone a bit mad. Even before that he'd tried to set fire to his daughter's wedding dress.

Franny Daniels is long dead as well. He did a lot of bird in his younger days. He was such a good-looking man when he was young; film star looks. You'd never take him for a top villain. He was there in the Mayfair Bridge Club in Mount Street when Glasgow hardman Jack Buggy got shot. I think Jack had actually been born an American but he was always known as Scotch Jack from the time he'd lived in Glasgow. Franny was part owner of the club. It wasn't really a bridge club, they played more kalecki there; they served tea and bacon sandwiches. Jack turned up a few days later in the sea off Newhaven and there was a great inquiry. Eventually, years later, Franny and a fellow from the club got done on the word of some Australian shoplifter who said he'd been in the club when Jack was shot, but I'm glad to say it got kicked out at the Old Bailey.

There was a lot of talk about Buggy trying to get back some of my friend Roy James's money from the Train which had gone missing, but it was protection pure and simple and Franny wasn't having any of it.

6 August 1998

In 1998, Marilyn wanted me to go with her to see Ronnie Biggs, the train robber, in Brazil. When it come to it I didn't go. I didn't want to. It wasn't the money and Ronnie's a smashing fellow but I'm nearly 75 and it's a long way. I'm much happier taking Danny, our dog, for a walk. She's had him since he was a puppy. Got him from Harrods, but now he's getting old like me and it's not fair to leave him with friends and it's even less fair to put him in kennels.

I've never been one for holidays really. For many years my summers were spent on the Isle of Wight. Funny though, I couldn't recommend the place where I stayed. There was no sea view from any of the rooms and in all the time I was there I never got to any of the beaches.

Because of my kind of work this sort of holiday was quite common, but sometimes I did get to go to nice places as well. I spent a long time in Montmartre in Paris once, when I was having a bit of trouble here and I needed to be absent. There's a nice picture of me on the Eiffel Tower. I did get to Coney Island when I was sent to do a bit of work in America in the fifties, but holidays, not really.

When Albert Dimes and Jack Spot had their big fight in Soho in the summer of 1955 Billy Hill, who was

Albert's great pal, sent me down there to do a bit of minding of Sammy Bellson, who called himself the Gov'nor of Brighton, so I suppose in a way that was a holiday. It was a wonderful town in those days, what with the all-night drinkers and spielers – places like Sherry's and the Bucket of Blood.

Then after Jack Spot got slashed the next year I spent a few days in Ireland. Billy Hill, for who I did the work, drove me up to Manchester and I got the ferry across from Liverpool. He'd rented a house near the bus garage where the Frenchman fought an Irish bloke for the world title, I can't think of their names now, but I didn't get out much. As I remember the weather wasn't too bad and there was plenty to drink, but foolishly I didn't stay long enough and when I came back I got nicked straight off the plane at London Airport.

That cost me a seven and when I come out from that Billy took me and a lovely man called Ray Rosa to the South of France as a thank you. We stayed in the Carlton in Nice where we had the best rooms and Billy had champagne laid on for us when we arrived. I remember we went on a boat tour to that island where the Man in the Iron Mask was supposed to have been kept and Ray and me shut the door on Billy in the cell. I thought it was a good joke but he wasn't none too pleased.

From 1965 onwards it was the Isle of Wight at best, and Dartmoor at worst, for my holidays. Even when I came out at the end of doing twenty years at the end of the eighties I didn't go away. I'd been away enough as it was. I had a few days in Brighton where I'd lived but then it was back to London quick.

I suppose I don't think much of holidays because I never got used to having them as a child. It was only when my father got £100 compensation, which was big money in the thirties, after losing a finger, that he took all five of us children to a B and B in Southend for a few days. Once I did go with the Catholics to a sort of farm run by monks, and a couple of years there was hop-picking where we could take Timmy our dog with us. You know the things you used to see on newsreels, everyone waving from a charabanc, a hut for your family and you shared the lavatory with another four huts, and singing round a fire in the evening. Dad stayed behind and worked.

I don't think I've been very lucky with holidays anyway. When I came out following the twenty years I did after the Torture Trial and the Parkhurst Riot, Charlie Richardson asked me to go and collect some money for him in Marbella over some property transaction that fell through. That would have been a bit of a holiday really. See some people, have a few drinks, pick up the dough and come home. What happens but I'm arrested and spend time in the nick over there. It was all legitimate because I got released and Charlie got his money back, but that kind of thing puts you off.

After my first book come out Marilyn wanted to go to Cancun in Mexico and we got a package there. Even then we didn't start too well and she got the rep to move us to a decent hotel. The one we went to first was dreadful for what we were paying and she had a ruck with the tour guide until we got moved.

I'm a good swimmer. I'd learned to swim in the Thames by what's now the Oxo building near Waterloo Bridge as a boy diving for pennies but I don't like going in the water now. When I was in the nick as a young man, to cut yourself was the fashionable thing to do and I slashed both my arms. I've eighty stitches in each and after all these years they still show. So it's a bit embarrassing if people look. On that trip when people asked me what I do I told them I wrote books and did bits on telly. Some people did recognise me and that was all right, but I wasn't going to say to people I didn't know 'I've just done twenty years'. It would have embarrassed them.

I don't mind being on my own. I can do whatever I like. If I want to walk Danny I can. I don't have to ask the governor's permission. I don't have to ask anyone's permission to do anything. So, in fact, after all these years of being locked up every day is a bit of a holiday.

8 August 1963

Overall, the Great Train Robbers haven't had much luck. They say it themselves that the whole thing was jinxed. Look what's happened to them. How many of them kept their dough? Roy James didn't and then he had that terrible row with his wife's family, got another stretch and then he died. Tommy Wisbey, my father-in-law as it were, even though he's the better part of ten years younger than me, got out of the case with Tina Meer, the girl supergrass who put Billy Gentry away, funnily enough over more thefts from trains, but then he went down with Jimmy Hussey over some cocaine. They both picked up a seven. He works on a flower stall now. Jim's disappeared from view. I don't mean he'd disappeared in any nasty sense but he's dropped out. The last time I saw him was at Roy's funeral. Gordon Goody's in Spain still. I suppose he's done as well as any. Bobby Welsh didn't really have that good treatment in prison when he had a bad leg. He had it off a few weeks ago, and when I saw him he said it felt a million times better. He was a good gambling man; knew what he was doing. If anyone could pick you a winner Bobby could. Jimmy White? Never heard of one way or another. He come from North London, a very talented man all round, very good with keys. One time he had a little café. He was the one hid his money in the panelling of his motor home and it took a long time for the coppers to find it. Roger Cordery's dropped from view.

Poor sod, Billy Boal, who got convicted of the robbery itself, was really a wimp and it showed. He should never have been convicted. How anyone in their right mind thought he'd have been allowed within a hundred miles of the train is a mystery. He only got roped in by Roger Cordery who'd known him when they were in Borstal together. That was the only bit of bird that Boal did, I think.

In a way I had it against him even before I met him. The ones who was really on it felt gutted for him and for Renee, his wife, and whilst they're all on remand they have some dough sent to her. What does he do but shout out in the dock that they're giving him money? Just the sort of thing you want the Pros and the bench to know.

I know the Court of Appeal quashed his conviction for the Train, but by then it was already too late. They gave him fourteen years for receiving the money with Cordery and he's not long into his sentence when he dies.

I did like Charlie Wilson but I knew him mostly through prison rather than out. His was another good escape and it shows how poor security was in them days. No one seemed to have learned any lessons from the escape of George Blake and all the tightening up after the Mountbatten Report. Charlie was in Winson Green at the time. And, by chance, the screws couldn't have made it easier for the men who came in and got him. They made him keep his clothes outside the cell. The men who came to get Charlie out had a passkey made from a screw's own key and they knocked down an elderly night watchman on their way in. The other night watchman was making bacon and eggs and that was all there was about. The trouble was they didn't know which was Charlie's cell but they didn't have to look far. There was his clothes in a pile outside his cell door. He was gone hours before anyone even noticed. Of course there was a nationwide search but Charlie was in a Birmingham flat until he went to Knightsbridge, where he waited until it was safe to go. It was seven months before he went abroad. He picked the name Ronald Alloway and went over to France and then to Mexico to see Buster Edwards and Ronnie Biggs, before he went on to Montreal. He was there until January 1968 when he got nicked. That copper Tommy Butler had overheard the conversation of one of Charlie's friends in which Canada was mentioned and he put two and two together.

Like a lot on the train, Charlie was a good South London boy. And like some of the others, after he come out in 1978 he went into drugs and got himself killed in his villa down in Marbella in April 1990 by Danny Roff. Charlie had already had a piece of luck. He managed to get out of a Pros for fraud by paying £400,000 to the Customs. Then he did four months on remand on robbery charges before they was dropped.

Roff lasted a good few years after that, before he was shot to bits. Then he got done in a club at the New Cross end of the Old Kent Road and somehow he survived. He was disabled, the papers said, but he was still able to get in and out of his car. Not fast enough though. They caught up with him in his driveway in Bromley and took him out once and for all. Roff was a good spender in clubs but he was related to the Carters and so I really wasn't bothered to know him one way or the other. He got in the Tin Pan before my nephew Jimmy, Eva's son, turned it into a wine bar. Ronnie Knight had it before Jimmy, as well as the A and R – Artists and Recreation it was called officially.

Georgie Stokes bought the A and R off Jimmy but what he did was he forgot to renew the licence and the authorities don't lark about nowadays. They closed it down. It's still completely empty – opposite the Astoria just near where Freddie Mills got killed all those years ago. Georgie then got nicked in a thing with cocaine in champagne bottles. He got a twelve and pissed off while he was on home leave. The last I heard of him he'd been nicked in Spain.

13 August 1964

Today was the last two executions in Britain and I don't
suppose now there'll be any more. Peter Anthony Allen
who was only 21 and his lodger Gwynne Owen Evans.
They'd robbed and killed a man in Workington, John
Alan West, at his home there during a robbery. They
stabbed him in the chest. He'd been a friend of Allen's
and used to lend him money and they knew he'd got
cash about the house. Of course they blamed each other
for who'd actually done it but it didn't do either of them
no good.

Funnily enough, the day they appealed was the first
time ever the courts had ordered a re-trial on a murder
charge but it wasn't theirs. It was a man named Isaac
who'd killed someone in a fight in a pub. If they heard
of his result they must have known it wasn't going to be
their day, because there's no way the court was going to
quash two murder convictions on the same day. In fact
it didn't do Isaac much good because he got a guilty the
second time as well. At least he didn't swing.

During the appeal they kept them separate in the dock
to stop them getting at each other and there was a whole
lot of argument about whether evidence that Allen
carried a knife was admissible. The trouble was it wasn't
the Pros who had put that bit of evidence in, it was Evans.

In fact they were a bit unlucky to swing. The Home Sec had reprieved a fellow called Masters who'd beaten an old man to death earlier that year, so they must have thought they stood a good chance. Maybe it was because West'd been a friend of Allen's that did for them. Allen didn't take the news well and he went and smashed the glass in the visiting room. They didn't let the prisoner and his visitors actually be able to touch. Allen got topped in Walton and Evans in Strangeways. Funnily enough the screwsman for Evans was named Allen as well, same spelling.

August Bank Holiday

August Bank Holiday in Brighton, seems like that Graham Greene film with the fight at Lewes races and Darby Sabini giving Richard Attenborough a lecture.

Once Spot and Albert had had their fight then Billy Hill sent me down to Brighton to look out for things. Sammy Bellson was the man in the town and he was really a Spot man but we soon converted him. What Hilly didn't want was Spot to have support. He wanted him isolated. Before that, though, I'd been down again for the races. I was on the joint giving the change out for Tommy Falco and Johnny Rice, who were looking after Albert's pitch for him whilst he was on remand. Packed, the day was, when I got a pull. John Sambridge who they called Happy – although he wasn't when I'd finished with him – pointed me out to that DI Careless who got done a bit afterwards over a false passport application. He upped and off to South Africa and when he came back he wrote in the *News of the Screws* how he was the target for The Syndicate in London and this is what made him go hooky. He got a small fine over the passport but the girl he'd done it for, the table tennis player Richard Bergman's wife, got fined about ten times as much for selling drinks after hours. But there again she didn't have a fashionable brief defending her.

Careless had that Bill Hemming, the ex-copper, who defended all the coppers in trouble in them days.

Anyway there was some story that I was down there to kill Jimmy Kensit, the actress Patsy's father. I wasn't. I don't say I wouldn't have done him if I'd seen him but I wouldn't have killed him. Kensit was sweet with Spot at the time so he was fair game. The coppers down there didn't know me and they had to get Sambridge to point me out. What a diabolical thing to do. I'd known him in Wandsworth in either 1947 or 1948 and he hadn't a good name then. I did him in that nick and I suppose that's part of why he went with the coppers.

All they did was give me a good talking to and tell me it would be the worse if they saw me in Brighton again. I could expect to be fitted up. And it was town enough for that to happen. It wasn't long after they did the chief constable, a couple of sergeants and Sammy Belstead for corruption. The chief constable used to ride up and down the promenade showing off on a white horse and he was lucky the jury disagreed over him. He even got his pension but he had to argue it all the way up to the House of Lords before he managed it. I had a drink with him a couple of times before he got nicked.

The man who done Sambridge with me in Wandsworth was Harry Hobley, a good thief come out of Camden Town, and he was married to Georgie Ball's sister. His son married a girl who was in *Coronation Street* at one time.

Over the years I did a bit of work with him. He was with us in Druid Street, Bermondsey, where Coalshop Harry had a snooker hall in the railway arches. Next door was a warehouse of stockings and clothes, things which were trumpy when there was rationing. Someone found out and we backed a lorry in. Stuttery Robinson, who got nicked with Billy Hill, was with us that day.

Then Harry's wife went off with some other bloke and had a kid by him and Harry couldn't handle it. He got a seven and was sent to Dartmoor where he just started chinning people for no reason. One day he lays one on Jimmy Essex, which wasn't a sensible thing to do. Essex wasn't someone you chinned lightly. The screws jumped in before too much happened and it was only a matter of time before Harry was on his way to Broadmoor.

That's where he died. I was in Chelmsford at the time when his boy, who was doing a two, told me he'd heard from his dad that they were poisoning him, but poor old Harry was well gone by then.

As for Happy Sambridge I caught up with him years later after I come out of doing the seven for Jack Spot. Someone marked my card where he was in London and I took his leg off with a shotgun.

2 September 1999

It's funny what people do. This evening I went on a signing of my books in Swindon. After a bit of a talk I answer questions and then I sign the books and have a chat with people. I don't mind if they don't buy the books. If they haven't got the money it doesn't matter. Very often they bring up a bit of paper or a serviette and I'll sign that. A lot of them want their photos taken with me and, of course, I'm happy to oblige them. Anyway this man has a paper bag and when he reaches the table he brings out an axe and says can he be photographed with me holding it to his head?

I couldn't hardly say no, particularly after he'd bought the book, but a pair of pliers would have been more appropriate. I wasn't ever a Mad Axeman. In fact the only person I ever chopped up was that Eric Mason, who interfered with me and Eddie Richardson after a bit of trouble in the Astor Club one night at the beginning of '64 or '65.

Eric wasn't a bad guy. I'd met him in prison but, in fact, I hardly knew him. I was down there when a fight erupted. It was nothing to do with Eddie or me and we just paid our bill and left. By now it was about 2 a.m. Then outside we bumped into Mason and a couple of other people with him. Mason started saying 'I'm not standing for this nor will the other people stand for it either'. By this he was meaning the Twins, who he was running for at the time.

He was like threatening us. So I popped him into a car with another man driving and took him south of the river where I really see to him. I stuck an axe all over him. Then I took him to the London Hospital, and dumped him in his underclothes, wrapped in a blanket on the steps.

When he got out of hospital he wasn't at all grateful for my putting myself out and taking him to hospital. He wanted the Twins to take action against me but they gave him a few bob and told him to leave it out. He was the last man to be flogged in prison and he went on to write a book, so good luck to him. I think I'd have been about the last man to be flogged after I attacked the governor in Exeter over a beating Jack 'The Hat' McVitie got from the screws, and got sentenced to the cat. They didn't do it because I'd been certified insane three times already and the Home Secretary thought it wouldn't look good to have a madman flogged. Not that I was mad like I thought I was Napoleon. It was just the violence.

There've been a few axe murderers in history. I suppose the most famous one was Lizzie Borden[1] in America, who cut her parents to bits. When I was younger there was a musical comedy about her with a

---

[1] 32-year-old spinster Lizzie Borden from Fall River almost certainly killed her father Andrew and her stepmother on 3 August 1892. One of the pieces of evidence in her favour was the lack of any bloodstained clothing. She must either have stripped naked before she killed her victims or possibly had assistance from either a housemaid or her sister, who also loathed the stepmother. After the verdict she continued to live in Fall River and died in 1927. There have been a number of theories and books about the case, including suggestions that the Bordens were attacked by a stranger and that Lizzie killed them whilst suffering from some sort of epileptic fit. See Victoria Lincoln, *A Private Disgrace: Lizzie Borden by daylight*.

song which went 'You can't chop your mother up in Massachusetts' which was where she did it. There was also that rhyme:

> Lizzie Borden took an axe
> Gave her mother 40 whacks
> When she saw what she had done
> Gave her father forty-one.

It was one day in the heat which must have got to her and put her off balance. Her father had remarried and she hated her stepmother. She'd tried to buy some poison and the shopkeeper had refused to sell it to her and when only her stepmother and father were in the house she did the pair of them. The axe got found in the woodshed but forensics weren't like they are now and they couldn't actually tie it to her. She did well in court, fainting when things were going against her, and she got a not guilty. Funnily she never topped anyone else after that.

There'd been some others earlier including that Scotch woman Jessie McClachlan.[2] She was a sort of skivvy working for an accountant, John Fleming, in Glasgow and another servant was found half clothed and chopped to bits. Some of the family silver was

---

[2] The 1862 McClachlan case is an early example of what was almost certainly a miscarriage of justice. There is little doubt the judge did what he could to help James Fleming, whom many believe was the killer, at Jessie McClachlan's expense. His motive was undoubtedly rape and Fleming had been admonished ten years earlier for the sin of fornication, something concealed from the jury. After the conviction there was a wave of public sympathy for McClachlan. It was felt, however, that she had deliberately concealed the murder and although her sentence was commuted, she served fifteen years before going to America where she died on 1 January 1899. In the face of public hostility the Fleming family left Glasgow. Again there have been many books written about the case. See, for example, Christianna Brand, *Heaven Knows Who*.

stolen and Jessie was found pawning it. She said she'd done it for her employer's father James. She got convicted but there must have been some sort of doubt because she was reprieved.

I suppose the most famous worldwide was the Axeman in New Orleans just before and after the First World War. There's still books and novels being written about him. I suppose he's their equivalent of Jack the Ripper. Some of the ones before the war were probably Mafia killings but it was never clear. People got grassed by others and were lucky not to get topped. There was one father and son got convicted, but fortunately the Axeman struck again whilst they was on death row which was lucky for them and they got released.

According to the books it was probably a man called Joseph Mumfre, who was the later Axeman. He was shot by Mrs Pepitone whose husband Mike had been killed by him. She got three years in the nick but what is certain there weren't no more killings.[3]

---

[3] The killings ran from 1909 until October 1919, the last coming when Pepitone was axed to death. The father and son on death row were Iorlando and Frank. They were not released until the principal witness confessed she had made up the evidence against them. See John Canning (ed), *Unsolved Murders and Mysteries*.

6 September 1943

I think the saddest case I ever came across was Johnny Gray, who also called himself Ryan. I met him in Wandsworth in 1943 when he was in his eighties. He'd been a boy soldier in India where he chinned a sergeant and got ten years. He would tell me about the old days and his memory was terrific. There was an absolute silence rule then and when you went to chapel on a Sunday you sat in your own seat with high sides so you couldn't see the other prisoners. You went there in file wearing a hood, with your hand on the shoulder of the bloke in front. You were led by the equivalent of a trusty who didn't have to wear a hood. He must have been the oldest lag there was. He could remember prisoners being able to watch a hanging in Stafford prison. After, they stopped them being public. I know the last public execution was in 1868. It was Michael Brennan, that Fenian who blew up Clerkenwell prison in an effort to get some other Fenians out, but say the execution in Stafford happened in the 1880s, then Johnny'd have been the right age to have seen it.

When I met Johnny he was doing the rest of a Penal Servitude sentence. He'd been given ticket of leave and come up from Dartmoor. The train dropped him off at Waterloo and he never got no further than the station.

He saw a suitcase and he couldn't resist going for it. He got fourteen days for the luggage and they revoked his ticket of leave. Then, on the morning he was due to be released, blow me if a buzz bomb didn't hit the prison. He wasn't injured. He just collapsed and died of a heart attack in reception.

21 September 1954

I was thinking the other day about who was the best and gamest I ever knew. There's no doubt in my mind that Billy Hill was the best planner there ever was. You've only got to look to his track record. Two big ones out of two – the Eastcastle job and then the Jockey's Fields bullion robbery – in four years. The bullion one is nearly fifty years ago today. No one seriously nicked and nothing recovered. No wonder the papers talked about the coppers fighting a master criminal. Airlines had offices in funny places back then, and Jockey's Fields is a little sort of mews running off the Grays Inn Road. The KLM offices were there and they were taking a shipment of bullion. Their lorry drove in, and right behind was a smaller van which reversed up so their tailboards were facing each other. One of Bill's men leaped across on to the KLM van and threw a couple of boxes of bullion on to the other and they was off: £45,000 in as many seconds. Of course, they turned Bill inside out and upside down but they never found anything. That has to make him the best putter-up in the business.

I think the best man I knew with keys was Jock Robinson who was known as the Fitter. The secret to keys is getting them off the punter, taking an impression and getting them back without his knowing. There was no one quicker to take an impression than Jock and, over the years, there've been some good men at it.

As for a screwsman Teddy Hughes from the Elephant must be the best I've known. All the best have come from round here. Edgar Wallace used to come and drink in the pubs looking for stories – the Elephant and Castle of course, the Alfred's Head and I can't for the moment think of the third. Wallace used to drink a lot with old Bill Brindle, Eva's father-in-law. As for Teddy I went out with him in about 1951 when I was quite young. I've been a screwer in my time but I'll never be remembered as one. All my convictions since the early 1950s have been for violence. The last one I had for dishonesty was twelve months for sus. Really, to find a conviction for screwing, you'd have to go back to the clothing coupons we tried to get out of Benfleet Town Hall back in 1945.

I'll tell you who was a good climber and that was Billy Benstead – married Alice Diamond's, the leader of the Forty Thieves shoplifters, daughter. He had long arms, like an ape, and he could climb anything. He was the scourge of Belgravia but the trouble was he was like 'Taters' Chatham and Ray Jones the Welshman, degenerate gamblers all of them. He'd lose his dough down a spieler, go out and do a drum, go back down the club, sling the tom on the table and say 'Count us in' and, of course, he do the lot again. He did Lady Docker's jewels, Gordon Richards, the jockey's trophies and George Dawson's gear and Billy Hill got him to give them back as a favour. That and to get the heat off. For a big man Peter Scott was a good climber as well.

There wasn't many wheelmen around when I was young. For a start there wasn't that number of cars and not everyone knew how to drive. Today, first thing you do when you're seventeen is apply for a licence, but then there was no real point. Roy James who worked on the Train, now he was a good man behind the wheel, so was Albert Baffy apart from when he took a drop before a job; the last thing you wanted was some copper doing you for drunk driving – they hadn't got the breath test then. A bit later again, Billy White from Hoxton, but I think he was related to the White mob from King's Cross, he was a good driver. He was with us on the Victoria Park job. Danny Allpress, Alfie's son, was another really good one. Both him and Roy James were up to motor racing standard really. Poor Danny got put away by the grass Bertie Smalls and though he worked a bit when he came out he got cancer, he was still young. Lilian Goldstein, Ruby Sparkes's girl, she was great behind a wheel, must have been one of the first. Funny, a number of girls took up driving. There was Sheila Porritt worked up in Manchester. Her father was Abe Tobias, good man up there; put a lot of work Billy's way.

What was good in the old days was if you had an MRE set. There was fifty keys in a set and if you went up to a car you could see on the ignition which number worked it. There weren't that number of imports in those days and so near enough every car had an ignition which fitted. If you had the full Monty, as they say today, then you had it. A set was worth a fortune. Anyone who had one and was willing to sell it could name his price. What you did was break into a good garage and the keys would be hanging up in the office. No one thought much of security then. They just weren't alarmed up. In through the roof and off with the keys. Then any car on the street was yours.

As for safes, I've always thought they were overrated. Every safe I was involved with was a disappointment. I know people who've had their safes emptied will say there was millions of stones in them, but how much of that is to gee the insurance up? Same with thieves.

Stands to reason. They're never going to say they worked all night on a safe and got nothing out of it. Most of them will swear blind they took thousands but, when it comes to it, I don't know more than a handful who took out much over two or three grand.

You'd generally have someone on your team who knew how to do a safe, which in the old days wasn't all that difficult. It was a question of getting it out of the building and to a slaughter where you could work on it. You didn't want to work on it in the building if you didn't have to. There was always the danger there'd be some busybody or someone who'd hear a noise. Getting it out, that way you was the master. If you had to work on the premises then it was the master of you. After that, like I say, the safe would go in the Union Canal; wash the prints off for a start.

I remember doing the Initial Towel Company down Clerkenwell with Billy Blythe, God rest his soul. We'd had the info that it was going to be a bit tasty and so we'd got a Scot down from Glasgow to help out. Same share as the rest of us and his exes on top of course. We tied up the night watchman and the Scot blew it all but what a fiasco. Not a thing in it.

Overall Jock Robinson was as good a safeman as any I knew and over the years I met Eddie Chapman, Johnny Ramensky, Paddy Meehan, the lot. But Jock was their equal and better. Then, of course, the manufacturers improved safes so eventually they became untouchable. I knew some fellows who would order new safes from the manufacturers' catalogues and work on them practising, blowing them but that was an expensive game. And by then no one kept nothing in them anyway. That was the heartbreaking bit. Those questions the *Independent* put to me. One of them was what was my worst nightmare. I said it was doing a safe and finding there was nothing in it. That's bad enough but then finding out there was millions in it; the boss's secretary done it and you bumped into her on the way in.[1]

Not the same with deposit boxes, though. There's always something in them. No point in having them if you're going to keep them empty.

23 September 1996

I was walking Danny the Dog round the Angel one day when this small man, not smartly dressed or anything, come up to me and asked if I was Frankie Fraser. There's no point in denying it and he went on to say he'd read my book *Mad Frank* and if he'd had it with 'im would I have signed it? I said 'Of course' and that's the truth. He said he was a film producer and he'd like to put me in a film he was going to make. Personally, I thought he was a crank but that don't matter. You meet any number of cranks about the place. Anyway, he asked for my telephone number and I give it him. I went back to the flat and told Marilyn and she said 'Do you think he's an escaped nutter?' But there was nothing on the telly about anyone getting out of Broadmoor and so I thought nothing more of it and then, blow me, weeks later one day, right out of the blue, I get a telephone call from a J K Amalou of Adventure Films. Can he send a car for me and Marilyn to come and talk about putting me in a film?

Until we got to the studio I really didn't believe it but it was dead genuine. Did I want the role of the Godfather in *Hard Men*? Of course I said yes, and then he said a bit apologetically did I mind getting killed at the end? I said that all Godfathers got killed at the end

Marilyn was also in it. She had to play a blonde floozie in a Maltese nightclub and she said it would come natural.

I really enjoyed it. We did three or four days' shooting in Greenwich. The real stars Lee Ross, Vincent Regan and Ross Bowman, were really good to me. They'd sit me down and go through the script with me and tell me what I should be doing.

There was a premiere at the Odeon, Leicester Square, the smaller one of the two, and I had to get up on the stage and say a few words. I said it's far better speaking in this mike than the one at the Old Bailey when you're on trial for murder and the audience loved it. The film did very well and it was bottom of the top ten being shown for a few weeks. You can still see it on the Sky channels.

The next film I did was called *Table 5*. That was a low budget film which we did in Soho where we all end up on a roof chasing a cheque for £6 million. That got shown in Leicester Square as well. There's been talk of my doing a number of other films and people send me scripts with me in a cameo role. There was serious talk of me doing a bit part in a film about Viv Rogers, the Newcastle hardman who got done on New Year's Eve in 1993, but nothing's come of it yet.

I only met him in the nick but he was someone to be reckoned with. He got shot with a .377 Magnum outside a pub in Wallsend. He was the one did Gazza's knee in a nightclub up in Newcastle. There were so many reasons given out why he got done you don't know which is right. If any of them is, for that matter. He was meant to have been dealing in drugs and had crossed up some families in South Shields. Some people said he was muscling in where he shouldn't and that's why he was offed. Then there was the story that it was over the death of a fellow, Andy Winder, who had got done in Tenerife three months earlier. The story was that he'd left money for a contract on Rogers which was only to be exercised after his own death. Who knows. One thing is certain: no one's ever been done for it.

24 September 1981

Billy Tobin was a brilliant thief. Funnily, although he come from South London I never knew him before he was in the nick. Of course I was away so much and he was that much younger I suppose there was no reason for our paths to cross. What he did was a series of armed robberies. The last was on 16 December 1980 when he hijacked a crane and was ramming it through the back door of a security van in Alleyn Park, Dulwich. He got shot at by a copper but luckily the bullet went through his coat collar.

He got put away by a supergrass Philly Herbert. He was very close to Tobin and he went bent on him just as he'd done with others. He'd just come out of a seven and Tobin was helping him and that was his reward.

Billy hadn't done much bird before. What he was good at was getting acquitted. Something like five times on big robberies, including the robbery at the *Daily Mirror* when a security guard got shot dead. Billy had a not guilty after a four-week trial that time. Even this last occasion was a re-trial.

I first saw Billy when I was in E1 wing in Wandsworth. It used to be the punishment wing but over the years there was so much villainy by the screws that they'd closed it down and it was moved to H wing.

They'd only use it as a spare if, say, there was a riot in another nick and they needed to transfer people somewhere in a hurry. So it was empty and that's where they'd put me. I wouldn't be on a charge but I could be kept there if the governor certified that me being in the general prison would be contrary to good order. And the governors were always quite happy to do that. It wasn't too bad, except there'd be a whole load of screws, but you could take your time slopping out. In fact by 1980 when my boy Patrick was in they'd bring him over and let him in the cell with me. Not every day, of course, but a fair few number of times.

Anyway it was one of the times I was in Wandsworth I saw him. My cell overlooked the exercise yard and if I got up and hung on the window I could talk to the men on exercise. Things were getting easier in nicks by now and so screws would let them stop and talk for a little while. Billy would give me bits of news and he offered to get me cigarettes. Funnily enough, although you could keep bumping into the same people over the years I never saw him again, until about three years ago when I was at a bus stop opposite the Borough Tube. He pulled up and we had a chat.

As I heard it, Philly Herbert went to Australia. Best place for him.

26 September 1962

This was the day Jimmy Fraser, my nephew, Eva's boy, was fitted up along with a few others by that bent copper Tanky Challenor and he got put away for it. It was all on account of a grass, Wilf Gardiner. Jimmy was said to be part of a protection gang along with Ricky Pedrini, John Ford, Joseph Oliva and Alan Cheeseman, blagging the strip clubs in Soho.

I'd known Challenor – he got his name from being in the Tank Corps. To be fair he'd been brave in the war and he got the Military Medal but that's about all you could say for him. When Albert and Gilbert France and me had the Bonsoir he came sniffing round, but it was all above board and we sent him on his business. Challenor had been going mad for months, if not years, and he thought he was a one-man campaign to clean up Soho. When he was in a court he made it sound like Chicago in the days of Al Capone and what was worse everyone believed him. The truth is that, as a straight person, you could walk about Soho much easier than you can today. In a way straight people didn't go to Soho anyway unless they was looking for something a bit hooky, like a brass.

This Gardiner had a couple of clubs, the Geisha and the Phoenix, and he'd also got a couple of convictions for running girls. What he did was he went running to Challenor saying Jimmy and the others were leaning on him. One night Gardiner runs out of the Phoenix, waves at a couple of coppers and has Ricky and Alan nicked as they're passing. Then they got fitted up back at West End Central. Ricky had an iron bar planted on him and Alan was given a flick knife. Johnnie Ford was the next. He'd had a lot of trouble with Gardiner and that same night he was nicked as well. Two days later they picked up Joe Oliva whilst he was driving along Berwick Street with a couple of friends and Joe said Challenor planted a home-made bomb on him. Our Jimmy was the last. He was just in the street and he had a razor planted on him. Later he tweedled it in court and said he used it in the garden for cutting banana stalks. Looking back he should have just stuck it out with the truth, but in them days who was going to believe a young kid against a war hero?

Challenor did them all for conspiracy to demand money with menaces – it was said to be a hundred quid – and possessing offensive weapons. Gardiner give evidence of threats, saying they'd damaged his car and they'd threatened to cut him if he didn't pay and that if he tried nicking them they'd shoot him. All the usual rubbish.

Jimmy got off the conspiracy but all the others went down and Jimmy got fifteen months for the offensive weapon. Challenor got all the praise from the press for breaking up this dangerous gang, and what's worse he got a licence to go round fitting people up. But, thank God, he did it once too often and the Court of Appeal quashed the convictions. By then Jimmy had done his fifteen months and in them days there wasn't any compensation on offer.

And Challenor went on and on. He did all this in front of other officers, who didn't stop him. Some cricketer who went to stand bail for his girlfriend was called a black ponce and Challenor started singing that song 'Bongo, bongo, bongo I don't want to leave the Congo' which was popular at the time. Then he did overstep the mark. He planted half a brick and gave a bit of a smacking to a straight fellow demonstrating against the Queen of Greece and it all came on top of him. The brief pointed out there was no brick dust in the pocket and so the guy could never have had the brick at the demo. That did for Challenor and a couple of other coppers with him. They all got nicked.

They held an inquiry why, if he was suffering from exhaustion and so on, he was allowed to continue on duty. The man who conducted it was the Pros in the Great Train Robbery. Jim give evidence at it but the man found just about everything in the police's favour and, what a surprise, it was no one's fault. Apparently he'd been doing loopy things for years, like standing on the table and walking home. Tommy Butler wrote a report saying what a good officer he was. The reason he shouted at people was because he was hard of hearing. Funnily no one in the force had realised his mental condition.

The poor bastards who were with Challenor went to the nick but he was found unfit to plead and had a short spell in hospital. After that I heard he'd got a job as a solicitor's clerk over South London.

30 September 1976

This was a really bad time for me and the family. I was in Chelmsford and they said I was inciting the other prisoners to a riot. What had happened was a guy from Norfolk – I can't remember his name now – who was doing a twelve, a grand man, was having trouble with some screws at the 'centre'. That was where they sat and watched the wings. It was a sort of half circle with two big and two small wings coming off it. You had to go through the centre more or less whenever you went anywhere, like on exercise.

When I heard about his problems I wouldn't stand for it and I kicked up murders on his behalf and as a result I got a right kicking. They held me down and gave me an injection and then I was put in a straitjacket and it was straight down the punishment block. When they took me out of the jacket I felt really awful but they kept on giving me a couple of shots a day. Somehow I wrote to Eva on scraps of paper and I managed to have them smuggled out. There's always someone who'll take a chance and help you, and in turn they or their family will get a bit of help from yours if they need it.

She kept them and gave them to the *Guardian* in case they could do something about it. I always took pride in writing letters home but this one was just on the back of bits of paper. It said 'They have taken a real liberty honestly Eve won't write anymore it is an effort to concentrate let alone write as they have injected me on 2 occasions yesterday dinner time and tea time and it is powerful stuff I feel absolutely terrible'.

Of course they fetched up to see me straight away. My nephew Jimmy, that's Eva's boy, drove her and my mother. I never ever wanted my mum to come and see me in prison, let alone like this, but this time she insisted. They didn't want to let them in the gate but it was visiting time and all the other families knew who they were and what was happening. Eventually they let them in to see me in a special room. If they hadn't the prison would have gone up. One of the wives or girlfriends would have told their fellow and it would have gone round like wildfire.

My mother nearly collapsed. She wasn't getting any younger and she confirmed to the paper that I had bruises all over my face and body. The prison was po-faced about it all. Some spokesman said I hadn't any injuries and I'd been sedated after being put in a body belt, which is smaller than a straitjacket. After Eva and my mother and Jimmy come to see me they didn't sedate me any more. I just got shipped straight out to Wandsworth.

I can't really describe what the sedation was like. You're in another world and it's frightening. Every so often you'd come round for a few minutes and then you'd go again. There was no sense of time or anything.

It was terribly sad Reggie dying so soon after he was released from prison. I'd been meaning to go and see him and one Sunday, shortly before he died, Marilyn said, 'Why don't you just go up?' So I got hold of Vince who drives some of the Gangland tours for us and he said he'd go straight up there with me. When we got to the hospital, I said, 'Come on in,' but he said he wouldn't feel comfortable seeing that he'd never met Reggie. I think he felt it would be an intrusion so he stayed in the car park waiting for me.

Reggie was on the fifth floor and I was just chatting to the nurse when out of the room comes Bradley Allerdyce who'd been inside with Reg, and he says, 'Miracle, Frank. I was just on my way to phone you because Reggie's been asking for you.' So I went in like a magician, threw my arms open wide and went, 'Da da!' He couldn't believe it. He was very weak of course but he wasn't too badly tubed up. He was saying how difficult it had been when he was under guard and how much better it was now they'd left.

He wanted to know how I'd got there and, when I told him Vince had driven me, he asked why Vince didn't come up and would I mind going down and getting him up so he could thank him. What a good gesture.

Marilyn and I went to the funeral, of course. Roberta sent a limousine for us and we were near the front of the church. It was a lovely service and we went to the graveside. We didn't go to the reception afterward. I don't think even Roberta did. The limo took us straight home.

But there was a nice surprise that day after all. At the graveside Bradley handed me an envelope with a letter from Reggie for me. There was a photo in it as well. Unbeknownst to me Bradley had taken a picture of us when I went to the hospital and Reg wanted to make sure I was given it when he was buried.

20 October 1969

It's the anniversary of the Parkhurst Riot today.

If you have a demo in prison the one thing the screws try and do is prey on the weakest of you and so weaken the demo by chipping away people who aren't wholly committed from the edges. It's funny how some strong men on the outside won't lead when they get in the nick. Dodger Mullins was one. He was a real tearaway outside but he wouldn't take part in the Dartmoor Riot. I know there's a Jack Mullins acquitted but that's not Dodger. This one came from up North somewhere. I've been in the nick with both of them. Nor would Charlie Kray participate in sitdowns during the summer of 1972. Nor would Alfie Gerard – and if ever there was a fearsome man on the outside it was Alfie. But no, once inside he seemed to be a pussy cat and it nearly got him in a whole lot of trouble over the death of Ginger Marks.

I was reading Roy Shaw's book the other day and he was writing about a couple of demonstrations he took part in at Gartree. He says he offered to break me out on one of them but I think he was only there the first one. The second one I was in the strong cell so I didn't see all of it.

The first disturbance was in the summer of 1982 and it was totally peaceful. In fact it couldn't have gone better. What happened was that six guys in the kitchen were slung out by the screw in charge. The food was dreadful in those days. Whatever we had for breakfast, and it was often goulash, was inedible so we sent it back saying we wouldn't eat it. The screw told the men to put the remains off our plates in the big fridge they had, so it could be reheated in three or four days' time, and they rightly said they weren't going to do it. That was when he sacked them. When they told us Roy and I decided to have a sit in.

Reggie Maudling, who Billy Hill had got into, was a very liberal Home Secretary so far as prisons was concerned and we were allowed out of an evening to sit around, play football or whatever before we got locked up for the night. By the time we had to go in, Roy and I had been round enough people and most of us refused. The potential grasses went in, of course, and one or two of the weaker ones followed them. On that yard you could talk to the people in the ground floor cells and they were making out they'd overheard the screws tell them forty screws were coming from Winson Green and another thirty from somewhere else. Of course, the screws had told them to tell us this to give us the jimmies. Then the screws said there'd be no punishment for those who went in right away, and a few did so, but Roy and I held the rest steady.

Next thing the deputy governor came out and asked what was the problem. Me and Roy told him and said we'd all go in if the men were given their jobs back. He said he couldn't do anything, but he come out again about two hours later. He said they would get their jobs back for the time being, that if we went in no one would be put on report, and that since it was so late no one would have to work the next day. There would be an inquiry and if the prison officer was found to be correct the men would get the sack again. We thought that what he meant was this was an end of the matter and there never would be an inquiry. There was a bit of a rock garden and Roy and I stood on the stones and told them that we thought in the circumstances it was a victory and we should go in.

The deputy was true to his word. No one was nicked; no one was hurt. But behind the scenes the Prison Officers' Association must have gone off alarming as to the slights to their kitchen officer.

I left the prison to go to Wormwood Scrubs to have another operation on my nose which had got broken in the Parkhurst Riot. Looking back I should have stayed there, but I wanted to go to Gartree – it was much better for a visit even though it was farther for Eva and Doreen to travel. I'm sure Roy had been moved to Hull by the time I got back. I got in another bit of trouble at Gartree and I was in the strong cell when the prisoners had another sit-out. It had become a regular thing across the country by this time. Maudling had said that provided the prisoners caused no trouble they were not to be nicked. It was a sort of proper legal strike. That was when they lowered the coffee into me. Someone had gone on the roof and had chipped a little hole in the gap under the window, but there was no question of trying to spring me. They'd have had to do a much bigger hole and they'd have needed a tank to make it. But I must have been the first to have hot coffee in the strong cell.

It's funny how close you can be to people and lose touch completely. It was like that with the Parkhurst trial. For a few months we were solid but now I've no real idea where most of the others are, let alone stay in touch with them. Probably it's you don't make friendships in prison which last on the outside. Timmy Noonan's dead now. He died in Ireland and Eva went over for the funeral. Billy Blythe I haven't heard of in years, thank God. He turned out a right wrong 'un. After he come out he began going with Shirley, Eva's daughter, and he turned out a right dog. He was another of poor old Shirley's bad luck with men; conned money off her rotten. I believe she even married him although, of course, I was away at the time. Mickey Peterson I was with in Bedford when he was on remand before he got a couple of years for a tie-up of a jeweller. I heard last year that he'd pulled a twelve over a big drug factory. I never heard of Micky Andrews again nor Mark Owens. As for Andy Anderson, who I'd helped when he got out of Wandsworth with Ronnie Biggs, he drifted into the King's Cross scene with some other Scots. I've never even bumped into him when I've been in Glasgow.

Stan Thompson was a good 'un though. In December 1980 he got out of Brixton with the IRA guy Gerard Tuite and my old mate Jimmy Moody. Stan was on trial at St Albans for a blagging and he can't have fancied his chances. When it came to it he needn't have bothered. He got a not guilty and now here he is on the run for something they've found him innocent of. In the end he gets his brief to take him into the nick. He has to wait another six months, though, before he gets a bender.

22 October 1999

I was watching that television programme about Mrs Duncan and the last witch trial this evening. Of course it wasn't really a witch trial, more of a fraudulent medium trial, but she was done at the Old Bailey under the Witchcraft Act 1735. I think she was the last person they ever tried for that offence.

I remember the trial quite well because I was in Wandsworth at the time in the prison hospital. Of course you couldn't get the linens legally, but the guy who cleaned out the rooms of the principal medical officer or the doctors sometimes managed to nick a paper. It wouldn't necessarily be that day's, but anything was better than no paper and he'd smuggle it in to me. If I had one weakness in prison it was that I did like the linens. There was no newspapers in the prison for the cons except for those on remand. Lots of people liked them, of course, but they wouldn't take a chance because with the prisons half-empty they had screws to spare and you could get searched every day. If they found you with a paper it automatically meant bread and water and a loss of remission and people were terrified – but I was game.

I was fascinated how gullible people were. What Mrs Duncan did was batten on to people who'd lost their loved ones at sea and who were presumed drowned, and say she could get in touch with them through the spirits. Of course, these poor people who didn't know what had happened to their relatives were only too pleased to pony up and give her a few quid if she could set their minds at rest that they were at peace. In that court case she told a naval officer she could get in touch with his sister. When he said she was doing well driving an ambulance she said, 'No, the other sister'. He checked out with his mother and there wasn't any other older sister. What seems to have happened is that this officer changed seats by accident with the person she'd set up for the info.

She was making a good living at it down in Portsmouth, getting a hundred plus a week which was really big money. It may have only been a pound or two or three quid a time, but it added up when you had all these people in a séance. She'd already been nicked up in Edinburgh for the same thing and this time she got nine months, which was quite a hefty sentence. The programme made out she was a bit of a martyr but that was rubbish. There were plenty like her in the war, going round giving false hope and comfort to people. They'd find out the relatives through articles in the local newspapers about merchant seamen and those whose bodies had never been found, or they'd have touts who'd supply them with information and they'd spin them a yarn. They were so plausible they convinced parents or wives that they were dead genuine, and once they'd got them they'd bleed them. Don't forget there was no TV, not many magazines and only the Home Service and the Light Programme and Radio Luxembourg for people to listen to, and people wanted to get good news. When people like her got convicted and we found out what they were in for they got a good bashing.

31 October 1941

This was the day they topped poor old Babe Mancini over the stabbing of Harry Distleman in the Palm Beach Bottles Club in Wardour Street. It was all over who had control of the clubs – what was left of the Sabinis and the Jewish element. Towards the end, Darby Sabini hadn't really been able to keep the Jews and the Italians separate in his firm. One lot was always wanting something more than the others, and when the war broke out the authorities took the opportunity to intern the Sabinis and Bert Marsh, whose real name was Papa Pasquale. They said these were dangerous men who, if there was an invasion, could lead an uprising. That was a bit strong, most of them had kids serving in the war and not one of them could really speak Italian. They had a Scotch mother and she was the one who had brought them up. There was talk that the Sabinis were put away because of the successful gold bullion raid at Croydon Airport which the coppers had never been able to pin on them.

Once the Sabinis were away the Yiddisher Gang began muscling in on the Sabinis' clubs and spielers and that's when trouble started. One fellow, Eddie Fletcher got a bad beating and that's probably the real start Anyway, by 1941 Babe Mancini was one of the few o the Italians left looking after their interests. Albert Dimes and his elder brother, Italian Jock, whose real name was Victor, were about but Albert, being a deserter from the RAF, was on the run so overall he wasn't exactly prominent. But he took a good part that night.

This Eddie Fletcher had caused some more trouble, earlier in the evening, and he'd had another seeing to. He'd gone to hospital and now he'd come back. He said to get his coat. Poor old Babe was the doorman at the Palm Beach that evening. It was a smart place and he was wearing a dinner jacket when Sammy Ledderman came and told him some people were smashing another club, well it was really a spieler, in the same building. So he changed and then he goes up to see what was happening. What he told the police was he heard someone say when he walked in: 'There's Babe, let's knife him'. Babe said that Fletcher started fighting and came at him with a chair, and once he saw a knife on the floor he picked it up to defend hisself. It's easy to be wise afterwards but these things are usually over in a few seconds. It's not like the films where fights go on ten minutes. You can get a real good straightener which goes on, but mostly it's first one in with the punch who wins. Albert and Jock were there and it seems like Jock was trying to keep his brother out of the fight. Little Hubby Distleman, who wasn't an angel himself, got stabbed in the chest and dies calling out 'Baby's stabbed me in the heart'. Babe got done for murder and Albert and Joseph Colette and Harry Capocci got done for wounding Fletcher. It was the usual thing. The Yiddisher Mob was fighting just as hard and they'd started the trouble, but the coppers had to pick one side or they wouldn't have any evidence.

Babe was very unlucky. The Pros would have taken a plea to manslaughter, but for some reason or other he fought it all the way. He had a good judge who tried to help him but down he went. He appealed and this time the judge got his knuckles rapped for being too helpful to Babe.

Where Babe was unlucky, Albert and the other two had a bit of good fortune. Once they'd had the murder trial no one really wanted to give evidence in the wounding and so the three of them got bound over to come up for judgement. Albert got sent back to his unit but he didn't last long. He was on his toes again within a few months and this time they let him go. The RAF was particular about who they had with them, even more than the Navy. The Army didn't mind who they had, provided they could march up to a machine-gun. Albert spent most of the rest of the war up in Blackpool doing a bit of business.

Distleman's bigger brother 'Big Hubby' died a very wealthy man. He'd run a string of brothels in the West End. People said he had over £4 million in safeboxes when he died. Sammy Ledderman who gave evidence against Babe was another thing altogether. He took up with the Twins and ended giving evidence against them as well. He'd been their barman in a hotel they took over in the Seven Sisters Road and he used to mind weapons for them. He had a flat in Cannon Street, with a piano in which he kept a gun, and he had a walking stick with a stiletto in it which he minded for Ronnie.

2 November 1999

I was over the Angel today, just by the park where I used to exercise Danny and where he found my gold chain. He was just rooting in the gutter and came on it. My wife Doreen had given it to me and I'd lost it. Couldn't find it anywhere. It had been with me all through prison and the clasp must have broken when I was out walking him.

Danny was a wonderful little dog. Marilyn had got him from Harrods when he was a puppy. Gina Lollobrigida had his litter brother. Danny was getting old last year and we had to have him put to sleep. The vet said he had no quality of life. He said 'Do you want to be present?' and if I'd known what it was going to be like I'd have said 'No way, thank you'. Danny must have had an instinct what was going to happen. He'd been quiet and docile in my arms but, when I went to hand him over, he fought like a tiger until they managed to inject him. It was a sad day. Marilyn cried her eyes out. It even made the vets cry. He was only the third dog I've ever had in my life.

There was Timmy, an Airedale, which we had when I was young and which my sister Eva and me used to take with us to get the stale bread from Soho and, funnily enough, the second dog I had was an

Airedale as well. I'd got one for Francis, my youngest, when we lived in Brighton. We just saw an ad in the *Argus* and bought him from a breeder about twenty miles away. Then it looked as though I was going to be nicked by Rogers, after he'd got me to set fire to a bingo hall in Eastbourne and then tried to knock me for the money, and I had to go on my toes for a bit. Whilst I was away the worry for Doreen was just too much, that and coping with a young puppy, and they had to give him to my eldest son, Frank, which meant he had a good home. I wouldn't want another dog now. It's too sad when they get old, and anyway I'm too old for another dog myself. There's some elderly Canadian millionaire who had a dog which died, and even though he could afford a thousand dogs he won't get another. Instead he goes to the local dogs' home and takes them out for walks. I know what he means.

Anyway I'd been back to the Angel, got a haircut and as I came out I thought I'd have a cup of tea in Alfredo's just off the Green. When I get there it looks as though it's been closed down. I know that the present owner, Vincent, and his brother, Victor, who lived over the top were talking about selling it and it looks as though they've gone and done it. Their father, old man Alfredo, started it in the 1920s. He was a great pal of Papa Pasquale, who fought as Bert Marsh before he got done for a murder at Wandsworth dog-track. Bert was a great friend of the Sabinis and he was the one who organised a brilliant theft of gold from Croydon Airport. Him and the Sabinis were interned in the war. There was rubbish about their being enemy aliens who might lead a revolution against the British. For a start they were only half Italian and most of them couldn't speak a word of it anyway. They were all brought up by their mother and it was their father who was Italian. There was always talk that them being interned was the authorities' revenge for that gold snatch.[1]

It was Alfredo who stood bail for Albert Dimes when he fought with Jack Spot in Frith Street in April 1955. That was called the fight that never was because, after Albert got chucked, Spotty got a hooky vicar to say that it was Albert doing the attacking. Albert was in Brixton for a few weeks but then, when it looked like he could get bail if he had a surety, Alfredo never even hesitated. He was a very good man. I suppose that's another landmark gone now.

---

[1] On 1 September 1936 Massimino Monte Columbo was stabbed to death at Wandsworth Greyhound Racing track, opened some four years earlier. A fight broke out in the 2/6d ring witnessed by Jim Wicks, who thirty years later was the manager of Henry Cooper.

The murder charge was dismissed and Marsh, as the older man who had a criminal record for assaults and unlawful wounding, received twelve months for manslaughter. For a fuller account of the case see James Morton, Gangland.

The Croydon Airport bullion robbery took place on 6 March 1936 when three boxes of gold and sovereigns were being held by Imperial Airways before being sent to Paris. Impressions of the keys to the strongroom were obtained and when the night manager, who was the only person on the airport overnight, went to flag in a German airliner the store was raided. A Sabini man, Silvio Mazzardo, known as Shonk, was convicted and sentenced to seven years. Two others were acquitted. See Frank Fraser, Mad Frank and Friends.

9 November 1980

This was a bad day for the family. Poor Shirley, Eva's daughter, got nicked for murder. The coppers came round one Sunday and there was a man's head on a plate in her fridge. Just like John the Baptist. She'd been drinking heavily and had got involved with this Michael Bowden, who was a few years younger than herself. She was on the rebound from that Blythe from the Parkhurst Riot who turned out such a dog. Bowden and another couple of mates lured an alcoholic up to Shirley's flat in Colby Street, intending to rob him, but things got out of hand and they ended up cutting him to pieces whilst he was still alive. The last thing Shirley remembered before she passed out was seeing them come into her room and hold his head up in front of her. They'd used a saw, machete and an electric carving knife on the poor sod. After they'd put his head in Shirley's fridge they put the bits of the body in refuse sacks and went and dumped it over on wasteland on another bit of the Elmington Estate. Then they went off for a Chinese meal.

They'd made a terrible mess, of course, and there was blood all along the pavement back to Shirley's front door so the coppers didn't have to be brains of Britain to know where to look.

I heard a story, I don't know if it's true, that his brief found this Bowden really difficult to deal with. He wouldn't give him any instructions and, just before the trial was on at the Old Bailey, counsel went to see him in prison to see if they could persuade him to tell them what his defence was. The senior brief put the Pros' photos of the bits of the body in front of Bowden and asked him if he could tell him anything. Bowden had a look and then said 'Yes sir, it wasn't suicide'.

In the end it came out well for Shirley. She got chucked by the jury and Bowden and the other two got life. It took well over a year to come to court. She got a bit of probation for helping to unlawfully dispose of the body, but everyone could see that it was nothing to do with her. For a time she got malicious telephone calls asking if that was the takeaway place and could she send a hearse, but fortunately it all died down. Her dad gave out a statement saying he was sure they hadn't started cutting the man up until he was dead and that seemed to help. Anyway Shirley's done well, stopped drinking and turned her life around.

Bowden escaped about ten years ago whilst they were transferring him from a prison. So far as I know he's still out, but I don't actually try and keep track of him. The only other funny thing about the case is that one of them was a gravedigger by trade, so you'd have thought they'd have known more what to do.

9 November 1999

I was going to see James Morton about the book this evening when I ran into 'Pats' Parsons who'd been in the nick with me. I get the bus from the Elephant, get off in Aldwych and then walk to James's offices and I have to pass the Law Courts in the Strand. There was Pats coming out. He'd been on the appeal of his brother, Brian, who's done ten years of a life sentence over the killing of an old lady. The Court had said it would give its decision later and Pats asked me what I thought. I said it had to be a good sign. In my day often the Court never even retired. They'd listen to what was said and the two judges on either side of the senior one in the middle would go into a huddle with him, whispering for about two minutes, and then they'd chuck the appeal. So Pat's brother must have had a chance. He'd been there as well. The case had been one of those on the new National Commission, which sends cases where there's some doubt back to the Court of Appeal for a re-hearing.

Mostly you never got to be in the Court when they chucked out your appeal. You had to ask permission to come and hear your case. It's still the same. The reason they give is there'd be no room for anything but prisoners in the court because everyone would want a day out. That and security, of course. Some of the greatest prison breaks have been whilst people have been on trial or at the Law Courts.

I reckon probably the best of them was Alfie Hinds from the Strand. He was running an action in person against the Prison Commissioners and he had to go to a hearing in the Law Courts before a master. A master's a sort of junior judge and in those days he gave orders when the case was going to be heard and how many expert witnesses there were for each person. The whole place is like a rabbit warren with stone stairs and corners galore. Anyway, that day Alfie managed to palm a key from the screw's pocket, pushes him in a lavatory and is off on his toes. He got clean out into the Strand, jumps in a car and is off to Waterloo before they can get the door unlocked.

Tragedy was that he was caught that night, getting on a plane in Bristol to fly to Ireland. The stewardess said later she felt mean about giving him away, but people was more spirited in those days. He'd had help from Tony Maffia, who they called the Magpie because he hoarded everything – gold, silver, coins anything he could get to keep – and Tony got twelve months. Later he got shot by that Stephen Jewell from Manchester in some quarrel or other, and got left in the boot of his own car outside a pub near Southend. There was something hooky about the whole thing because Jewell went and surrendered to that crooked copper Ken Drury. He got life but until the day he died he never stopped protesting about how innocent he was.

As for Alfie it was back to prison again for him, until he managed to get out again from Chelmsford in 1958 with a duplicate key. This time he made it to Ireland and he was out two years until he got nicked once again.

12 November 1999

Today when I was in the King's Head on the corner of Walworth Road just near where Manor Place Baths used to be I couldn't help thinking how different pubs are from when I was younger. Fifty-sixty years ago people drank more. There was no giant telly to watch the racing on. Three o'clock was shut down, and that was when we were off to the spielers and drinking clubs. Three-quarters of the guys who'd have been here in those days would have done a bit of bird, and they'd have been looked on with awe even if they'd only done two or three months. If someone went to prison then it meant they would not get a job, simple as that. First, there wasn't the employment there is today. Now if you want to work you can get some sort of a job, even if it's only stacking shelves in a supermarket. Back then if you'd done a bit of bird there was no chance of getting a job. It didn't even have to be bird for dishonesty. Take 'Mad' Alfie Hicks, who was Tommy Steele's uncle. He had form for steaming into coppers and he couldn't get a regular job for years. Then, 'Mad' was a sort of mark of respect. If you went into coppers you were always mad because of the beating you'd get, even if you'd only slung a right hand and missed.

In 1946 they had a 'Spivs and Drones' outing from this pub. Spivs in those days were those who sold bent gear, black market stuff. Spiv was meant to be VIPS in reverse and drones didn't work. Anyhow they had a trip to Brighton for the day and when they all got back they'd been on the piss all day and there was a right ruckus. There were murders. My memory is that two people got killed. Crashed their heads on the pavement or whatever. Bobby Oakes, who was with me in Portland Borstal, got done but I'm glad to say he got out of it. Sitting here brings back memories.

In fact it was just down the road from here that Eva's husband Jimmy Brindle got done for a screwing at the Duke of Clarence in 1940. There's a brand new police station there now. He, Whippo and Tommy Brindle, along with Jimmy Robson and Billy Holmes, all got caught lifting the cellar flaps to get Scotch out. The road was being repaired and it was marked out with sort of hurricane lamps and they did the copper with one of them. That's when Jimmy came to Feltham Borstal in 1940, which is where I met him and that's where he met Eva when she come to see me. After that they kept meeting each other – they were local, of course, and it just went on from there.

17 November 1998

My wife, Doreen, died. She was still living in Hove where we met. She was ten years younger than me and that made her sixty-five. She'd been a heavy smoker all her life. She'd tried hard to stop smoking but like Billy Hill and many another she couldn't. She had cancer. What can I say about her? She couldn't have been better to me and she brought up Francis wonderfully all alone. I was away for almost all the years he was growing up. I don't think she missed a visiting day unless she was ill. And all the troubles the screws put her through – threats of strip searches, being knocked to the ground in Lincoln when I was getting a beating in the visiting room, and she burst in to try and see what was happening.

Even though we'd been separated for some years we still were friends. I've said before it was hard for her because she didn't come from a criminal family, which would have made life that much easier. I'm not sure she was ever really the same after her mother died but no one could have done better for me.

22 November 1981

This was a good day for the family. Frank junior and my nephew Jimmy had been charged with the Williams & Glyn's bank robbery on 28 September 1977. Now the DPP dropped the charges for a second time. What had happened was a brilliant stroke by George Copley who'd been done with them. They didn't call him Colonel for nothing. What he done was get a tape recorder into his cell and when he was being interviewed by a copper he had the machine on. The copper wanted to strike a deal with him. Of course this couldn't be allowed and so no evidence was offered. The Pros said there were 'certain irregularities'. What happened was the coppers gave evidence about the interview and lo and behold when the tape's heard it's nothing like.

Jim walked out and Frank had a bit left to do on the five-year sentence he got for Operation Carter and handling some stolen tom. Frank had been on bail at the time of the robbery over the Bank of America and that got dropped as well. Him and George got three years apiece for robbing a jeweller's down Stepney way. They were on bail for that at the time of the Williams robbery and the papers had something to say about why these men were given bail in the first place. George and Frank had also got a couple more robberies in 1976 and

'77 when they were meant to have done the Midland for forty grand. Everything dropped.

It was the second go the police had had. The first time there was so little evidence the charges were dropped, but because they hadn't been in front of a jury they could be brought again. It was always said £55,000 of the half million or so the robbers got went to bribe the police about evidence but I can't say anything about that.

In fact I hardly knew George – after all, he was my boy's generation, not mine. He come to see me once in the nick. I never even knew what relation he was to Cadillac Johnny Copley who got killed in a chase across Tower Bridge. Cadillac Johnny's sister had a baby by Johnny Parry so Johnny Parry Jnr is Johnny Copley's nephew. It was Johnny Parry senior who, all those years ago with Henry Cohen, set up a brilliant stamp fraud which they let us in on. Johnny junior got ten years for handling some of the Brinks Mat money. I did a bit of minding of Brian Perry in that trial; just be around to give him a leg up, so to speak.

23 November 1999

I was watching that film *Man Hunt* with Walter Pidgeon on the telly this afternoon and what struck me was not just how the stars weren't ever without a cigarette, but that they always wore hats. Men and women. We all did in them days. A lot of faces wore hats indoors as well. That was because they were going bald and were so vain they didn't want anyone to know. Jack the Hat was one, of course, and Jimmy Essex was another, so was Billy Blythe. They didn't like going to places like the Astor because they were made to take them off then, so instead they'd say 'Let's have a party' and take some crates round to a flat. That was so they could get to keep their hats on.

Harry Mellaship could have played the part Pidgeon had in that film. Harry was a very handsome man indeed, looked like a top copper; always wore a hat. But he didn't need to keep it on indoors. He was a conman who conned his own. I used to see him quite a lot in the Gun in Spitalfields, where I take people on my tour and in the Primrose which has gone now. He was a pal of Albert Baffy who I did a lot of work with. Before the war Albert was a famous driver. Then he got a five with a guy from Camden Town whose name I can't remember, so I don't suppose Albert was on the top of his form that day. In fact sometimes Albert wasn't on top form at all. I remember once meeting up with him and Patsy Lyons at my sister Eva's place in the Great Dover Road. We were off to do a job and Patsy caught Albert having a drink from a half bottle of Scotch. Gave him a right slap as much as to say 'Behave yourself. We're working'. Albert said nothing. He realised he'd been in the wrong. It's sad Patsy became a bit of a wrong'un at the end of his life because he was a good thief. He was far too close to Charlie Mitchell, who grassed the Twins.

One day round about February 1951 him, Jimmy Ford and Freddie Adams, who was called Fairy although he wasn't one – light on his feet I suppose – did a window in Sloane Square. An off-duty cop steamed into them and Jimmy done him. It was real bad luck that the copper taught boxing to a boy's club where Jimmy had been so he knew him. Jimmy went on his toes.

He'd been at Dunkirk, brave soldier and a good man. He'd had the birch at Lewes in 1942 for doing a screw. What he told me was that whilst he was on the run Harry comes round dressed as a copper, mackintosh, trilby and had a buck playing the sergeant with him to blag money off Jim. That was the type of crook Harry was. It was a fairly common blag in them days. Provided the victim didn't know you there wasn't much trouble. You knew someone on the run or who'd got a load of false tom and you went round to arrest them. Waved a brief at them – they never looked twice if you had the presence. Then your buck would take the man in the corner and say he could do something with his guv'nor and money would change hands. The other version is for a buy to be raided by false cops who are in with the sellers. They confiscate everything and split it later. The mug punters are just pleased not to be nicked. It's something cops have done as well over the years. Really it's only a version of that trick they pulled in that film *The Sting*.

Harry used to take care of himself and that's when he got cut badly when he was getting on a bit. Every morning about seven he'd go for a bit of a run down the Lea Bridge Road and a Scotsman, Billy Quinn, did him. I don't know what it was about. Harry wouldn't press charges but Quinn still got a three. For his pains Quinn also got a duffing from the son of one of Harry's friends.

Poor old Fairy Adams topped himself in a Cardiff hotel one Christmas. It was around '73 or '74. He'd been with birds but he never married, never had a family and it must have got to him, but who can tell? He'd have been in his seventies.

3 December 1979

They found Dukey Osbourne's body on Hackney Marshes this day and again, like Charlie Taylor, his is one of the deaths which have always been a bit of a mystery. Did he have a heart attack? Was it an overdose? I'd known him a long time both in and out of the nick. Some people even say he topped himself but others aren't so sure. It may have been a drug overdose but no one's certain. What does seem likely is that the body got put in a deep freeze before it was put out to grass. I didn't realise it at the time, but he turned out to be a bit poufy. He also had a rug, which I didn't know either. I worked with him in the early 1950s and he was a good man then. I know him through Jimmy Humphreys and he was a friend of Dukey. We did a wages snatch and a couple of other things together. I didn't see him a lot after that. I should think the last time I see him outside the nick was early 1965 before I got nicked over Dickie Hart.

What I did hear was that he'd gone in with the Twins. The story goes that he was from some public school and he'd owed them money from some gambling debt. As a result they'd got him working for them, keeping their guns for them. The first bits may be right but, like I say, he'd been at it for years before the Twins ever left school. Dukey was clever, there's no doubt, and he did a bit of snout dealing in the nick. I don't know where he met up with Lennie Watkins but it eventually did for both of them. They started importing high grade cannabis from Pakistan but this Watkins, the moment they'd had the first run, started showing off; lighting cigars with £20 notes, just the sort of thing to attract attention. No wonder they called him 'Silly Eddie'. Last time they went on a run they had Freddie Foreman with them. What they didn't know was that the Customs was shadowing them all the way and he couldn't shake them off. When he stopped in the Commercial Road one of the Customs went up to the lorry and Lennie shot him point-blank. An old age pensioner knocked Lennie down with his stick.

It was six weeks after this that Dukey was found dead. Some people said he'd died under questioning about where some drugs were. Lennie got convicted and there was a failed escape attempt when he was in Winchester. Someone saw a ladder up against the wall. Lennie eventually topped himself.

Freddie was lucky again. He wasn't Prossed with the others and got chucked later on.

4 December 1990

In the early days I think he was just a wannabee,
wanted to be a name and, in fairness, he became one.
Got out of murder with Gus Thatcher and then he got a
fourteen over some robberies. He escaped out of
Kingsdown in Portsmouth, did a jeweller's at Brighton.
Finally he got caught doing a job in Burlington Arcade.
The brothers who owned the shop went after him and
he fired at them, but I don't suppose he was so quick on
his pins because they tackled him and brought him
down. Then out of the blue he went and confessed he'd
killed Alan Roberts, his partner. Shot him by mistake
when the raid on a jeweller went wrong. Shot the
jeweller as well. That was the end of him, of course.
Threw away the key.

I suspect he'll be back in Portsmouth Prison where
they keep all the oldies now. Before the war it was an

old Preventive Detention prison and then it was a Borstal for many years. It was also a dump for licence revokes. Whilst I was at Dartmoor I knew a screw who came from there. His brother had done a bit of bird and as a screw he wasn't a bad bloke as they go. Bit of fellow feeling.

Then Portsmouth became a first-time star offenders long-term prison. But now it's for elderly lifers. Reggie Kray thought he'd be going there. It's a bit of an easy place and so it should be. Even since I came out last in '89 prisons have changed more or less out of recognition. Now there's TVs in the cells. I think that's marvellous. It would be a life-saver. You can have a telly sent in or you can even rent one off the prison. In my time for long periods I wouldn't even read a book. I wouldn't want to show any weakness where they could hurt me any more. Trouble is now you're banged up two and three in a cell. You had your own in my day except when something went seriously wrong, like during the war and the bombing. Then they put you three up to stop the homo thing.

The difference now is in the visits. For a prisoner it's the humiliation – even taking your socks off after a visit.

I went to see one of my sons today; jacket off, tie off, shoes off, dogs and a machine all over you. It's the drugs, not an escape they're trying to stop. To escape from a closed prison nowadays would be miracle. Outside of someone not returning from home leave you couldn't even think about it. Screws love all this searching, smirking all the time particularly when the women concerned are the old mums.

It was about three-quarters of the way through my twenty years around 1979 that drugs started coming into prison, passed by mouth. That was the way then. Now you've got to have a screw straightened. What with closed circuit TV you couldn't get them in on a visit. You could years ago, go to the toilet and put it up your

deaf and dumb. The visits themselves are smashing, far
better than I ever had and much longer. The screws are
miles away but there's CCTV in the rooms. Any visitor
who manages to give the prisoner something deserves
to win the lottery. But that said, there's more drugs
washing around prisons than there ever has been.

10 December 1987

I reckon the best-ever escape from a British jail has to be the one Sidney Draper did when he got out of Gartree. I knew him, of course, and Johnny Kendall who got out with him. Johnny had been a member of the Hole in the Wall Gang, which just rammed lorries into warehouses. He'd already got away when he was being taken from Maidstone to Parkhurst in November 1984. His mates did exactly the same thing – rammed the prison van, broke the windscreen and pulled Johnny and another man out. Johnny was out the better part of two years before they got him for a string of robberies and threw in an attempted murder for good measure. They put him in Gartree to await trial on this new lot.

Gartree was a funny place. It was one of the first super security prisons of the time. It was out in the countryside away from everywhere. Market Harborough's the nearest town of any size and the prison had no high buildings. Like many other new prisons it had a football pitch, but this one was well away from the buildings themselves. When it started out there were two massive fences but no wall. Then someone tried to tunnel out and they sprayed the outer fence with concrete. Albany on the Isle of Wight was the same.

In 1966 one of the train robbers had been up on the roof at Gartree protesting about conditions and a man from the press hired a helicopter which got very near, to try to have a talk to him. You'd have thought that the authorities would have learned from that but although there was a study done, when a senior officer said there was a real risk that someone could get a helicopter in and out, no one seems to have believed it. The only thing they did have was a connection to the local RAF base, which was supposed to be able to send up some fighter plane in a matter of minutes. They called it Rogue Elephant but I'm not sure if it was meant to shoot the escapers down. I don't believe anyone had thought that through.

There'd been plenty of goes at escaping from Gartree but it was Siddy Draper who had the brilliant idea of being sky-lifted. Andrew Russell did a trial run and then he hired a helicopter from Stanstead and said he was working for a security firm and wanted to sus out from the air places where lorry hi-jacks could take place. Up he goes and he sticks a gun in the pilot's neck and tells him to land in Gartree. Siddy and Johnny got a lot of help from other prisoners, who made a crowd to keep the guards away, just like they done in Wandsworth when Biggs escaped. The pair of them had towels which they waved at Russell so they could be recognised and they hopped into the chopper. It all took less than half a minute.

Some screw or the governor telephoned the airbase but it didn't do any good. No one seemed to have heard of Rogue Elephant and they didn't seem to know where Gartree was anyway. The screws were told to phone the police. Meanwhile they had the pilot put down on an industrial estate where they split up. Sid went off on his own and Johnny and Andrew went in a van. Then they forced a car off the road and took it over. After that they kidnapped an old man and tied him up in the back of his Metro in Sheffield. They left him forty quid for his trouble. It's funny. You'd think with such an elaborate escape they'd have had cars parked ready to go rather than having to do these snatches.

John didn't last long on the outside. They got both him and Andrew in a flat in the King's Road in Chelsea at the end of the following January. When Johnny was brought up at court the Pros said that he was far too violent to be brought into the dock so the beaks would have to go and see him in his cell. When they got there they found him being held down by a pile of policemen, calling out that he wanted to be taken up into court and, to their credit, they agreed.

When he was asked if he'd anything to say he told them a man in a coat with a pair of pliers had been yanking at his head. Of course it sounded as if it was me but I was in at the time. What the police was doing was taking a hair sample under the new Act which had come in. They just hadn't told him.

Sid Draper had a much longer go at things. Originally he'd been nicked over a raid in which a night watchman had been killed in Glasgow as far back as Christmas 1973 and was doing life with a twenty-five year recommendation. Sidney was a member of the Go Anywhere Gang and he and Billy Murray, whose father had been at school with me, went on this wages snatch at an engineering works. They'd already done a number of banks and this one was set up by a Robert Kennedy, who called himself Marley. The security guard went for them and got shot. The coppers, including Jack Slipper who went after Ronnie Biggs, got hold of Marley's girlfriend and then when he came home they nicked him as well. He started talking and it was only a matter of time before everyone got a pull. Young Billy Murray got away till after the Christmas and Sid Draper got caught near his pigeon loft.

Given the search that was going on for him after that helicopter escape you wouldn't think Sid Draper would have lasted any longer on the outside this time but he did. He stayed out until February 1989, when he was seen in Enfield where he'd met a new girl and the police picked him up there. The three of them came up at Leicester Crown Court and Sid got four years whilst John and Andrew got seven and ten respectively. All to be added to their sentences.

I didn't really know much about the escape. I was down in the punishment blocks most of the time and although I heard bits and pieces people could bring me, I didn't really get proper news.

As for Billy Murray I knew his father very well. We grew up together in the Walworth Road. He only did two bits of bird. The first was when he was about 20 and he got a Borstal. He went to North Sea Camp and I was there at the time although he was a bit older than me. You could get Borstal up to the age of 23 in them days. After that he got himself a job on the railways and he wasn't in trouble until sometime in the war he got six months for nicking stuff. After that his elder brother, Teddy, who was working in the theatre, got him a job as a scene shifter and he was never in any more trouble. One of his other sons still works in the theatre.

Billy Murray junior eventually got parole and then they pulled him back for not reporting often enough. He's out now. So's Alan Brown, another member of the Go Anywhere team, only in his case it's rather different. He kept applying for parole and kept getting a knock-back. The last time they told him it was going to be another four years before he could re-apply. He's already on a work scheme where he leaves prison every day and helps out in a café run by the church in Edinburgh. One day towards the end of last year he simply walks off during his lunch hour and hasn't been seen since.

I knew him quite well and when Marilyn and I went to Arthur Thompson's funeral we popped over to see him in Barlinnie. When Alan escaped there was a lot of talk in the press about how his old East End pals would help him but if he's still in the country I'd be very much surprised. Not that I know, of course.

12 December 1966

This was a big day in British crime. First Harry Roberts, John Duddy, who was a copper's son himself, and John Witney, who'd grassed them up, got weighed off for killing them three coppers in Shepherds Bush.

Of course I knew Harry and the others well in prison over the years.

At about 3 p.m. on 12 August 1966 some coppers stopped the three in Braybrooks Street, Shepherds Bush, near Wormwood Scrubs prison, West London. Witney had a Vauxhall with an out-of-date tax disc and the coppers wanted to talk to him about it. The trouble was they'd been off to do a rent collector and they was all tooled up and couldn't risk a pull.

It seems like two of the coppers went over to them, leaving the third in their own car. One of them was talking to Witney through the window and Jack said to Harry 'Let the slag have it', and Harry went and shot him in the face with a Luger. The second copper started trying to get back to the car and Harry shot him and all. The copper got up and then Harry shot him again. The third one tried to drive off but he ran over the second one and couldn't get away before Harry shot him and all.

A passer-by saw them drive off and thought there'd been a prison break. He got the Vauxhall's number and it was traced to a garage in Lambeth rented to John Witney. When the coppers called he said he'd sold it the previous day but they wouldn't wear it. He put up the names of Duddy and Harry and they got John Duddy in Glasgow in double quick time.

Harry was on the run for three months before he was found in woods in Hertfordshire. He'd been trained in survival in Malaysia in the army so it was easy for him. That they ever found him was a bit of bad luck as well. The police had picked up a pikey, who they thought quite wrongly had nicked some stuff and he told them about a campfire he'd seen in the forest near Bishops Stortford. Harry had taken to going further and further afield for his provisions, and whilst he was away the police found his fingerprints on a gun in the tent. They found Harry asleep in a barn.

They didn't hang around in those days. Harry was picked up on 11 November and they were all weighed off in a month. That wouldn't happen today. They all got life with a recommendation that they serve not less than thirty years.

Harry's other trouble was that in November 1958 he'd gone and robbed a seventy-nine-year-old man who died a year and three days after the attack. Had he died two days earlier the Pros could have brought a murder charge, but then if the victim lived a year and a day after the attack you couldn't. So Harry got seven years but it wasn't something the authorities would forget.

John Duddy died in the nick and Jack Witney was released in the early 1990s. He'd been a grass in the nick as well. He informed on them when they were trying to break into the PO's office and get the records. He was meant to be in on it but he went sick that morning. The pressure's been kept up on throwing the key away for Harry. It hasn't helped him either that he's become part of a football chant.

Harry Roberts, he's our man
He shoots coppers, bang, bang, bang.

You can still hear it sometimes.

Once Harry nearly got away from Parkhurst with Wally Probyn. They were working at it for weeks making replica guns but Harry went and left them in a lavatory. The screws found them and that was that. Even if they'd got out I doubt they'd have lasted long. The Isle of Wight was a bit like Alcatraz; the currents around the island were so strong no one could swim and they can shut down the ferry easily. You've got to have good outside help. In fact there've been very few escapes. I think there's only been one person ever get off the island.

I read in the papers a bit ago that someone had done John Witney, down in Bristol. It seems like he'd had a quarrel with a neighbour. Best thing that ever happened to him.

The other thing happened that day was Frank Mitchell, the one they called The Mad Axeman, got away from the Moor. I'd been in the nick with him over the years and as everyone knows the Twins sprung him. If they'd asked me, which wasn't likely, I'd have told them Frank was the last person they should ever think of springing. From what I knew of Frank, once he got out there was no way he was going to go back under his own steam. If he had done he'd probably have had to do twelve months more before he was given a release date, but he wouldn't have been able to see that and no one could have told him.

The story put about was that the Twins had got him off the Moor to act as a sort of equaliser to me in case real war broke out between them and the Richardsons, but there was never no real war likely. Both Charlie and Eddie Richardson were doing well in business at the time, and so was I – Eddie and me had fruit machines all over the country – and there was no need for any trouble. By the time they actually got him out I was doing five years and so was Eddie, so there was even less reason. I think they did it for prestige. Some of their firm wasn't as happy as they'd been in the past and this was a coup.

Frank was as big a man as I'm a small one. Big strong man, absolute giant he was, but really he was a gentle giant until you started to mess with him. But Frank had a lot of trouble in his life. He could write a fair hand but he wasn't the brightest of people and he'd been in special schools. First bit of bird he done when he was about 21 – he'd done approved schools and a Borstal of course – he had a bit of trouble with a crooked screw who'd nicked him for talking in the pouch shop in Wandsworth. After that it was the screw's big claim to fame. It give him a bit of a swagger. The screw had been a temporary in the war. Most screws were exempt from call-up but some went anyway, and they got temporaries in with the promise the regulars would get their jobs back at the end of the war. But when it was over some wanted to stay on in the services and some had been wounded, and so this one was one of those who'd been made up into full time. The screw eventually had his comeuppance. There was an article about him in the *People* and he sued for libel. Like so many of us it didn't do him any good. They fought it and he had to resign.

But, as for Frank, he couldn't handle discipline. Once he thought he was being treated unfairly he was off. He just got into more trouble in the nick until they put him in Rampton in 1955. He escaped two years later and he'd threatened an elderly couple with an axe whilst he was on the run. That's how he got his name. He got nine years for that.

I first met Frank whilst I was in Wandsworth in 1953. Him, Alfie Marks and me did a grass together. He was called Harry Cowans and he'd been the driver on an armed robbery at Nottingham. They'd cleared the better part of forty grand. I don't know how he got nicked but when he was he grassed up his mates. Anyway, one morning Alfie Hinds, Frank Mitchell and me were on Governor's Applications when the screws brought Cowans passed us. They said he was being brought to the prison stores to get a fresh pair of socks, but since he worked in the laundry he could have had any number of clean pairs if he'd wanted, so I don't know what that was about.

When we saw them coming I asked Frank and Alfie what we should do and Alfie didn't want to know. I didn't let Frank near Cowans but he piled in when the screws started to drag me off him. Cowans was a big man but he got a right hiding before the screws pulled me off. For good measure I did one of them too and so it was two months' loss of remission for the grass, five for the screw and 15 days No. 1 diet followed by 29 No. 2. By the time I came out I was transferred straight off to Durham and I never saw Frank again.

Funnily enough I did see Cowans and it was only the other day. I went to visit my boy David and there was a man in the visitors' waiting room who said 'Hello, Frank'. I said 'Hello' back although I couldn't place him, but later I asked who he was and David told me. I said 'He's the bastard I got time over, who I done in Lincoln and wound up doing a screw'. When the visit was over Cowans come over to shake hands and I said 'Piss Off'. He said 'Ain't you forgive us yet?' and I said 'Get out of it' and spit at him.

After that time in Lincoln he'd got twelve years or something like that over a security van and this time he hadn't grassed but that don't carry no weight with me.

As for Frank he was a right handful when he got sent to the Moor until the governor gave him a bit of freedom and he was allowed out on an outside working party. Thought it would calm him down and give him a bit of hope about a release and it did. But the screws were frightened of him. He didn't have to do any work. He was allowed off to pubs and the Twins sent him girls down from time to time. Then this day he just walked away from the working party and never came back. The Twins had a car waiting for him and he was back in London more or less before the real hue and cry went up. They put him in a flat and got a girl, Lisa, who was a hostess from one of the clubs, to stay with him but he got restless and wanted them to get him a release date before he would surrender himself. When they couldn't do this straight away he started threatening them. And that was something he shouldn't have done but he didn't have the intelligence to realise it.

Anyway, on Christmas Eve 1964 Albert Donoghue, one of the Twins' top men, told him he was going to be moved to a new address in Kent and that the girl Lisa would follow him. He was put in a van and had a few in the nut. Donoghue said Freddie Foreman and Alfie Gerard did it but I'm glad to say Freddie got slung, even after what he's been saying about Reggie and Ronnie on the telly. So did the Twins, even after they'd gone down for Jack the Hat and Georgie Cornell. Alfie was off somewhere in Australia at the time and he never even got charged. As far as I've heard Lisa the girl went to America and got married.

13 December 1999

Today's my birthday. I share it with the comedian Jim Davidson but he gets his name in the papers and I don't so often. Usually I dread my birthday. I've been nicked both in and out in prison so many times on my birthday I can't count. Mike Dalton threw a surprise party for me in Cleethorpes; a boxing dinner really and I was guest of honour. It was sponsored by Terry Smith who lives up there, got a scrap metal and demolition business. I really didn't know it was going off. Marilyn sang right out of her skin. It was really good.

In their own ways my sons have all been great boys even Francis jnr who's never ever been in a day's bother in his life; just joking. He's Doreen's boy, good boxer, played for Brighton and Hove Albion till he did his knee. He's been working in the City ever since. The others have been real chips off the old block. The sociologists could have a great time working out whether it's me or their environment or poverty which has turned them to crime, but they've all done their fair share. There's a story going round that when I was planning some job Frank jnr started crying and I held him by his heels outside the window of our block of flats. It's a good story, but like so many they tell of people it's not true.

As I write this Frank's in High Down. He got four years and four months in July 1999 over a bit of puff – quarter of a kilo I think it was. He got three in 1965, same year as I went away for the twenty. He was done over a post office van. He did thirty months out of that three because he went and chinned a screw in Maidstone. Then in 1974 he got a twelve months; and he was nicked but got out of the second go of the Bank of America. There's a film of the coppers raiding his house in the television documentary they did on Operation Carter. He got out of the really serious things but they found some tom behind a false wall and he got a five. He went off to live in Spain after that and he didn't get nicked again until the puff. Somewhere along the line he also drew a four.

Poor old David got a seven, when he was nineteen, over a security van. He finished that and almost at once he got half a stretch. In fact he's had so much bird I can't really count. I was in Wandsworth in July 1984 when he got fourteen years for the tie-up of an Arab banker. That was a ready-eye. They never stood a chance. The night he drew his bird the screws allowed him to come to my cell for us to have a chat for ten minutes which I have to admit was decent, and then, as I say, they did let us see each other about once a week until he got sent on. That sentence got knocked down to a twelve.

Then David got eight years in that case with the crooked copper and Kevin Cressey. That was hard. At the magistrates' court the case had been slung out because the Pros wouldn't disclose the evidence they had, so David went off to Spain. Whilst he's there he gets nicked for a dodgy car and a gun. He gets chucked on both those but by then the Pros is trying to re-open the case back here. They managed that and to get him extradited and he wound up with an eight. The judge wouldn't take off all the time he done in Spain and we went to the Divisional Court on his behalf but they said we should have appealed. When we appealed they said it was too late. He's in Spring Hill now and so, with luck, when this book comes out he'll be out with it.

Patrick's the youngest and he's done a handful including an eleven in 1980 over a security van and a fourteen over some cocaine. That was a funny business.

And the next generation? Well, Frank's son Tony is 26 and, like his uncle Francis, he went to a decent school and has never been in trouble in his life. I can't say the same for Patrick's son, Paul. He was a good boxer. He fought for England as an amateur but he's only a lightweight and he had the sense to know that however good he was there wasn't real money as a pro and it was better to do a bit of bird than have your brains beaten out. He's done a few years for puff also.

All in all I've eleven grandchildren and five great grandchildren. Most of the others aren't old enough to keep the flag flying.

16 December 1999

The Court of Appeal turned down Brian Parsons' appeal today and they got very stroppy with the journalist who'd done the investigation which had led up to it. Back in November 1987 Brian had been convicted of beating Ivy Batten to death at her bungalow in Shute in the West Country. The Pros' case was that she'd been hit seven times with a hammer by a burglar who dumped the weapon and a pair of gloves in a nearby field and they were found a week later. The old girl was 84 and she was known as The Railway Lady because, like the kids in that film, she waved to passengers on trains that went by her house.

From the moment he was arrested Brian always maintained he was innocent and he complained from the dock he'd been fitted up and his life had been ruined. Usually you'll get someone to say to the papers 'Oh yes, he had a bad temper' or 'I always sussed he had a bad side to him', but it seems there was nothing like this with Brian. He'd got no previous and the locals couldn't believe it of him.

From then on he'd fought to have his conviction quashed. The first time he was in front of the Court of Appeal was in 1980 and they slung him out but this time, like I say, he'd got the Commission behind him.

Apparently a story kept on going round that the gloves had been found by a police officer who'd not thought anything about them and then he'd put them back in the field so they could be re-found. There wasn't only that – the defence said that there was something like 160 items of evidence withheld by the Pros that they'd not known about.

The journalist and a London copper who'd also given evidence saying he'd heard the rumour got a right hammering, to the effect that they'd made it all up. The Court said that the investigating officers had behaved perfectly in every way and there was no suggestion they'd misbehaved at all. At one time the brief for the Pros asked a witness if it wouldn't be strange if a police officer picked up a hammer with blood on it and kept it in the boot of his car. It would be strange but it wouldn't be impossible, because those of us who've been around long enough can remember that's exactly what happened in that Towpath murder all those years ago, when a copper took a chopper home with him and used it to cut the firewood.[1]

So poor old Brian's got the rest of his life sentence to do. His trouble is going to be that if he goes on saying he's innocent the authorities are going to say he's not come to terms with his crime and he won't be given a licence.

---

[1] Alfred Charles Whiteway was convicted of the murder of Barbara Songhurst on 31 May 1953 on the towpath at Teddington. It was alleged he had attacked his victim with the axe found in the rear of a police car in which Whiteway had been sitting. The officer had taken it home, used it as Fraser says and, when realising how important a piece of evidence it was, handed it to another constable. Whiteway was hanged on 22 December 1953.

17 December 1990

There's always something good about seeing a bent copper go down. The trouble is it doesn't happen often enough. But one of the real dogs was Rodney Whichelo. He got done for demanding money from supermarkets. What he did was threaten to poison dog food and demanded the makers pay over £3 million into building societies. He also spiked jars of baby food with razor blades and rat poison. What he did when he was caught was try and blame it on his fellow coppers. He'd learned it through some police training he'd done, studying a case when someone tried to get money off that turkey king, Bernard Matthews, in the same way. He got seventeen years.

Of course he'd spend his time on Rule 43 along with the nonces and the grasses. Back in the days before they had that he'd have gone to a first offenders' prison like Wakefield, even if he'd got life. Even so they'd be closely watched. They'd get a soft job like in the library or an office or cleaning the officers' mess, things like that. As time went on and prisons got more crowded they had recidivists but then they'd have them in another wing and soon after that Rule 43 came in.

If Whichelo'd been in the general nick he could have expected a regular bashing and he'd have deserved it.

Whilst he was in the nick he went to court to try and get his pension back. Michael Howard had ruled he should lose three-quarters of it and the court said he was right. It was like that Chief Constable I used to drink with in Brighton, when I was down there minding Sammy Bellson. He got done but the case was chucked and he had to go all the way to the House of Lords to get a ruling he'd been unfairly treated by the Watch Committee and he could keep his dough.

In fact I think I only ever met one copper in the nick and not segregated. He was doing something like twenty years. His marriage had broken down and one day he asked another copper to give him a lift home and invited him in for coffee. Shock, horror, there's his wife dead. Like so many, though, he'd made a mistake. He'd smashed a window to make it look like a burglary but he'd smashed it from the wrong side. If you smash it from the outside most of the pieces will fall outside. You'd expect a copper to know that. He'd been having an affair with a WPC and when it came out she doubled on him too. Of course he made sure he never got near me.

Whichelo got out in 1998; said he was sorry and wanted people to forgive him. One good thing – the police started to look at some of the cases he'd been involved in and at least one guy, Chickie Matthews, no relation of Bernard, got out.

19 December 1964

I think everyone believes that Ronnie done 'Mad' Teddy
Smith down in Kent over a boy. But a funny thing
happened today. When I'm in Chancery Lane I often
buy a paper from the stall just by Cursitor Street and I
got talking with the fellow who runs it. He was telling
me that this wasn't so.

Teddy Smith was a bit of a pouf, big drinker but he
wrote stuff for the radio and telly and he had a play
called *The Top Bunk*. He got done with the Twins when
they tried to get Hew McCowan, who was another pouf,
to sell them the Hideaway Club in Gerrard Street –
which had been the Bonsoir when me and Albert and
Gilbert France owned it. It was a nice little place: no
hostesses but there was a band and a cabaret. I
remember we had Alma Cogan sing in it once.

Anyway McCowan who, to be fair, had got a bit of
guts in him wouldn't do it. This night Mad Teddy
comes, he's drunk and has a fight with one of the
waiters, starts throwing things around and did about
twenty quids' worth of damage. There was other problems. Opening night, a table's booked for ten people and
none of them shows. Now the place could take 100, so
ten's the difference between a decent profit or none at
all. Next time McCowan sees the Twins they point out,

quite rightly, that they could stop this sort of thing whether it was Teddy or someone else. McCowan thinks they're trying to put the black on him and goes to the police. This is just what Nipper Read, who's been told to try and get the Twins, wants and he nicks them and Teddy along with them. It all unravelled for him. Witnesses went bent on him and it turns out McCowan's been in the bin. That really does it. The first jury disagreed and the judge more or less told the jury to throw it out second time around. Not a stain on Teddy's character. Same night they went and bought the Hide-away from McCowan and called it the El Morocco. They threw a huge party with all sorts of film stars, like Edmund Purdom who was very big at the time.

Anyway around the time they finally get nicked it looks as though Teddy's disappeared and the rumour starts that he'd been done for. No one knows for sure, but these rumours gather pace and even the place in Kent gets named, but Ronnie's never nicked for it.

Anyway this paper seller tells me that Teddy's done the sensible thing when everyone's been nicked and he goes into hiding with this fellow's dad. He had him for about eight weeks and then Teddy goes up North or somewhere. The man's dad saw him again in 1972 and Teddy said he was off to Australia. He wouldn't be the first to have gone that route. If he's right, and he should know, it shows what a danger it is convicting people without a body.

21 December 1999

It's funny how things turn up. I was doing a signing in Waterstone's in Oxford Street this lunchtime when a geezer comes up and has a few books signed. Then he comes back and says he's an actor in an experimental theatre and they're putting on a play that evening in Battersea. Would I like to appear as myself in a walk-on. He'd pay exes and make sure I had a lift home so I said 'Of course'.

He turned out to be one hundred per cent genuine. One of the actors wanted his wife's lover dealt with and this guy said he knew just the man to give advice. I came on and said 'Well you have to shoot in the orchestra's or the thin and thick'. They gave out they didn't know what it meant and so my line was 'In the balls or the prick' and everyone fell about. But the real curious thing was who gave me a lift home.

After the signing, me and James Morton had been walking down the Charing Cross Road because I'd said I'd point out the A & R Club, which Ronnie Knight and then my nephew Jimmy had owned. It's looking completely derelict now but it's almost opposite the little alleyway where Freddie Mills was found shot dead. We were talking about his death and James was asking if I'd ever seen Freddie box and did I think he'd committed suicide or had someone taken him out?

In fact I'd seen him when he was at the top of his career just after the war when I come out of Liverpool. In those days there was really big boxing in London. You had to give an arm to get a ticket to a show at Harringay or Earls Court, which was where the big bouts were staged. The trouble was, though he had the heart of a lion, Freddie's technique wasn't all that great and he was fighting men who were a stone and more bigger than he was. He'd lead with his chin and he could take a punch. Nowadays you might not think that giving a stone away was over much, but just after the war and during rationing when people were smaller it was. Don't forget Sir Henry Cooper wouldn't really be a heavyweight now. If he was, neither him nor Rocky Marciano could last against these great big guys. It was the same with Freddie. He was only a light-heavy but since he beat them all he was often boxing heavies such as Bruce Woodcock, who wasn't all that bad himself. And he was getting a hammering.

Now who do you think gave me a lift back from Battersea after the show but Freddie Mills's stepson, the son of Don McCorkingdale from Chrissie Mills's first marriage. He pointed out where his grandfather, Ted Broadribb, who'd been Freddie's manager, had been born in Sheen Street, Walworth near the East Lane market. In fact I'd known Ted. He was one of the chaps. Much, much older than me, of course. He'd have been old enough to be my father.

I remember Ted saying when he'd taken someone to New York a guy had come to see him and said his boy would be paid such and such, which was half what had been agreed. Ted'd said he would pull the boy out rather than take a cut in wages and he'd been told the geezer was a Mafia and he'd be sensible to take what was being offered. Ted went on to manage Don McCorkingdale, and he later became secretary of the British Boxing Board of Control.

Now Don himself wasn't a bad boxer but he wasn't in the class of Freddie. Somehow it got so that Don's wife Chrissie started seeing Freddie and eventually she got a divorce from Don and they got marrried.

When he come out of the ring Freddie was so popular – about as popular as Henry Cooper and Frank Bruno when they retired. You'd see him on TV in things like *Six Five Special* and he did a bit of panto. Goodness knows how many shops and fêtes he opened, although whether he got anything for them over and above his exes who knows. He'd got the Chinese restaurant in his name. He did ringside commentaries and then it all seemed to start to slide away and go wrong on him. He was starting to get headaches from the punches he'd taken in the ring.

By the end Freddie was in all sorts of trouble. The restaurant wasn't doing good. The waiters was running a racket so that a plate of sandwiches cost nearly £20 and it went into their pockets not Freddie's or his partner's. Freddie started a libel suit and then had to drop it. There was also some trouble about brasses being in the place. The other tragic thing is that Freddie was at least half an iron. People couldn't admit it in those days and things got covered up more than they do now, but he was very close to the TV singer Michael Holliday who'd topped himself a bit earlier. In 1965 he was found shot in his car in the alleyway by his restaurant. It looked like he done it himself because a few days earlier he'd borrowed a rifle from a woman who worked the fairground at Battersea. But no one wanted to believe it of Freddie. If he done it himself there might be trouble with the insurance because in them days companies didn't pay out on suicide. It was a crime. Well, not suicide itself – because there wasn't anyone to prosecute – but attempted suicide was. You could get a few months for it and, anyway, there was the disgrace of it for the family. It looked as though you was mental.

So a rumour grew up that the Twins wanted his place and when he wouldn't hand it over they'd had him done. It was a load of cobblers. The Twins never topped anyone who wasn't of their world and they'd never have topped Freddie. They were both boxing fanatics and idolised the old fighters like Freddie and Joe Louis and Sonny Liston. He was one of their heroes. There were even two investigations into his death. One when he died and another when Read was looking into the Twins. Like Nipper Read says in his book, he would have been delighted to have pinned Freddie's death on Ronnie and Reggie, but to be fair he has to say there was no suspicion let alone evidence against them.

The other funny thing about Freddie was there was always a rumour that he was Jack the Stripper: the name they gave to the man who killed half a dozen brasses down Hammersmith way. The first was in February 1965 and they ended about the time Freddie topped himself. Most of the tarts were naked and there were flakes of paint on their bodies. One or two had their teeth pushed in, and it looked as though they'd been plating someone when they got done. The official story was that a 45-year-old man who was a security guard who worked locally topped himself, leaving a note saying that he couldn't stand things any longer – but his name was never made public and there was this story it was Freddie who'd done them. Read, in his book, says he was horrified that there was even a suggestion that Freddie had been the one and that's what we all like to think. But, like I say, rumours abounded in the underworld and people say he was questioned, but rumours are as strong in the underworld as they are in ordinary life. I suppose nowadays if anyone bothered they'd be able to do a DNA examination and find out who it was for sure.

25 December 1999

At first the only things that made Christmas Day different from any other in the nick was that we had plum duff, which Winston Churchill instituted when he was Home Secretary at the time of Sidney Street. You thought it was wonderful. When I first went in the nick there was still people about who remembered the first time they had it. Dinner itself was just like any Sunday dinner, floating fat, but the cooks really did work hard on the duff.

Then there always was that George Arliss film shown in the chapel and sometimes there was a Christmas tree in the centre bit where the wings started. Later, in Wandsworth, after dinner about 11.30 in the morning, when we were locked up before the film, the Salvation Army band came and played. That went on for years but after we were allowed radios it seemed to fade away. There wasn't the need for them any more. Even later on, over the years there might be some concert with a woman singing at the piano – opera stuff not a singsong we might have liked. But only people on stage could go. Them that had served three months or more.

The screws were a bit better I suppose. We still were expected to do our cell tasks and if we hadn't then we could be on report – bread and water, loss of remission

– but Christmas Day they was a bit more lenient. You were expected to catch up on Boxing Day, though. There was a sort of truce. They wouldn't spin your cell for the week leading up to Christmas. Then there was always some crooked screw who'd bring in a bottle of Scotch. He wouldn't dare do it during the year in case he got searched, but Christmas he'd take the chance he wouldn't come a tumble.

At the end of the 1980s, when I went back for two years for receiving them coins, I didn't join in. I had my radio and it didn't worry me. I was in for two Christmases. The food had improved. Dinner and tea was better, even breakfast. There was a film show and they'd retired George Arliss but I didn't bother to go. The beds were better. At first they were a board on the cell floor, then they had little legs, but by the end of the 1980s they were really quite high off the ground – slats of course. You can't have no wire springs in a prison.

Even then, although I had only two to do, it was still war. You could have papers sent in but I didn't bother. When I did there'd be a screw say 'Yours hasn't come today, Fraser', or there'd be a couple of pages missing. I used to pay for some other guy to have one. That way I knew I'd get it clean and on the right day. And I made sure that Doreen and Eva sent in every letter Recorded Delivery.

If you were in prison outside London or the Home Counties you suffered. Freddie Foreman in his book says the screws and the others in the nick called you LGs – standing for London Gangsters – and it wasn't meant respectfully. He was right. The screws would do what they could to humiliate you and make you have a go at them and then put you on report.

In the old days just think of the villainy people would do for a dog end. They'd sell their food. Eventually we used to have a sort of duff pudding once a week and not only just for Christmas. Absolutely solid it was, but it was a change and it was very popular. What people used to do was arrange to sell their duff. Food was served at the door of your cell and you were then banged up right away, something like two hours or more before you were unlocked – and the man would be looking at the duff the whole time which he had to hand over during recreation. Often the temptation would be too much and they'd shave a bit off and eat it, and then a bit more and a bit more, and eventually by the time they handed it over it was more like a sugar lump. That would cause ructions.

Billy Carter was the youngest of the family who had this long-running vendetta with the Brindles and eventually with me. His mother had a cleaner's job in Whitehall and she'd bring all the dog ends home and take them down when she next saw him in Borstal. It was the power of tobacco. He could sell them and it meant he didn't have to sell anything else such as his food. No one thought there was anything unusual just 'Blimey, what a good old woman. What a shrewd idea'.

Christmas at home wasn't really much when I was growing up. Since he was half Red Indian it meant absolutely nothing to my father literally, but it did to Mum. We had to go to Midnight Mass, of course. But Christmas itself wasn't the present-giving there is today. I read this year that people spent an average of £900 over Christmas. I know there's been inflation but you could buy four or more houses for that when I was growing up.

It wasn't my parents' fault we didn't have many presents. We were like most other families – it was cheap and cheerful. In a way it was sad. There were these people wanting to do things for their kids and they just couldn't. We had a good Christmas dinner and we had the presents after that. I remember Mum got hold of an old piano for my elder sister Kathleen who was musical. I remember she first picked out the notes with one finger and then she got good – self-taught, she was. The tune she learned on was 'Gee, oh gosh, Oh Golly, I'm in Love with Molly'. Later, we'd have singsongs. It wasn't nothing having a piano then. Families made their own entertainment. Lots of poor households had one which had seen better days. But Mum and Dad didn't really have money to spare for decorations or Christmas trees, and if we had one it was because I nicked it from Covent Garden where the flower market was, just the other side of the water from us. I'd tell my mother I'd been given it after sweeping out a shop or running errands, something like that. She wanted to believe me. If we had a turkey it was because Eva and I had nicked it. I remember Billy Murray, the father of the guy who did life for that murder up in Scotland with Sid Draper, and me nicked a Christmas cake one day. It was from a shop in the Waterloo Road called David Greggs. You could lift the window up from the outside and that's exactly what we did. It was about 7.30 one evening. People saw us doing it and they never tried to stop us, they just gave us a clap and a cheer. I suppose I'd have been ten or eleven at the time.

Eva was with me on a lot of jobs. There was only one time she was with me when I got caught and she tried to get me away. I'd do the creeping and she was the lookout. Mainly we'd do offices. They all had safes then for petty cash and keys and so on. We'd just have the cash and away. We did nick a load of stamped labour cards once. Got clean away and when we realised that we couldn't do nothing with them we chucked them down a drain. A few weeks later we did the same drum and this time I was nicked. Eva rushed in saying I was her young brother and I was really looking for work, but when they questioned us we realised what they wanted was their cards back. They let us out on our promise to get them, so Eva held me by the heels and I went down the drain to try and find them. I got too heavy and she had some men passers-by hold me. She said I'd dropped Mum's money. People were incredibly naïve, no trusting's a better word, in them days. Well, the cards was still there and we took them round to my grandparents and dried them out in front of the fire. My Gran was a bit bad sighted and probably thought they were cigarette cards. They were in a bit of a mess even with the drying out and so we just chucked them in the office doorway. We didn't fancy meeting up with the men there. We thought they'd nick us once they'd got their property back.

Eva and I would walk all over London; get a tube out to Kensington. In York Road there was a set of emergency stairs for Waterloo station and we'd go down them. Not many people realised they were there. We'd be up and down them and once we were in it was easy to say we'd lost our tickets if we got stopped by a man at the barrier. People accepted that you had to have a ticket to start the journey and there weren't often jumpers on the train. If the worst came to the worst the guy collecting tickets could be distracted, and even then there was the sob story if all else failed. What we were doing was stealing from offices mainly, but if I could I'd get work sweeping a yard or something for half a crown and then, of course, I didn't touch the office. Sort of protection although they never realised it.

Mum may have turned a blind eye but my father never knew that's for sure. She was so upset the first time I got taken to court. She came with me but she kept it from my father. He'd have taken the belt to me. He'd have gone to town on me. Not in a cruel way but for my own good. Towards the end of her life my mother realised what we'd done to help things out and we often had a good laugh about it.

27 December 1970

So far as I can tell this was the first time in living memory anyone had been killed in a shoot-out with the police. The poor sod was Bobby Hart, no relation to Dickie. He was known as Bob the Barber because he liked cutting hair in prison. He cut mine and all. He'd started life as a barber. He come from Camberwell and he had the most awful luck you could ever wish on a man. He wasn't a bad thief. His speciality was doing cash raids on hospitals disguised as a doctor and he'd got three years for that back in 1964. He'd also done a three for handling. When he got shot he was doing the Nat West in Kensington High Street. It's all going sweet until they run out of the bank and there's a copper on his way to do guard duty at an embassy, and he shoots it out with them. Poor Bob was found in a Beach Buggy on the fourth floor of a multi-storey car park. He'd bled to death. Even worse luck, the copper had actually applied for a transfer to another force and it was one of his last days on duty.

Some other good men have gone down since that time. Mickey Calvey was one of the first. His old woman Linda was a wild one. She was known as the Black Widow and topped Ron Cook when he was out on day work. She'd been minding his money and when he come out it wasn't all going to be there. She got her new bloke to do him, but he couldn't bring himself to shoot old Ron so she did it herself. I heard she'd married this new geezer in the nick but I'd be careful about things if I were him. Then Nicky Payne and Mickey Flynn went down in Plumstead when they were after a security van, and after that Derek Whitlock copped it in North Woolwich.

Terry Dewsnap was another. He was related to Joe Wilkins by marriage. He'd done a good bit of bird. Back in the 1970s he'd been in a team that kidnapped a bank manager and his family and held them overnight out in Dunstable. Then they took the manager to the bank, made him open up and as the staff came in they put them in the vault. They made a tidy few quid out of that. Terry went off to Spain after that. Next thing the police have done Terry's son-in-law. What they couldn't believe was that he had a cast-iron alibi. He'd known what Terry was about to do and he'd gone round the local shops and into the local police station reporting his car missing all through the night. Terry didn't get picked up till much later and, by then, they let him plead guilty to receiving. He got shot over North Harrow way when he and Jimmy Farrell were doing a post office.

Of course, that's one of the reasons for going into drugs. You don't have to go near the stuff and chances are if you do, you won't get shot.

31 December 1999

I still get asked, say a couple of times a month, to do a bit of work but I turn everything down. People who know us properly do it very diplomatically but some of the offers I take with a pinch of salt. There's always the chance of someone being slipped in to you like they did with poor old Charlie Kray. In this last month alone I've even had two offers for me to oblige someone.[1] They was offers I didn't have to think twice to refuse.

It wouldn't really worry me if I had to go back in the nick again. With sons and grandsons who've kept the family flag flying I think the prestige would be tremendous. I think I'd be like a God even if I didn't have their reputation behind me. The books will have helped because I've never relented. I've never bent. No one's been able to smash me or to brainwash me. In my books where I think someone's done wrong I've said so.

But if you want to ask me any questions you can always find me on my website and I'll be happy to answer them. I had one the other day from an ex-screw at Rampton; asked did I know where Johnny Mangan was. I was hard put to remember who he was, let alone where. He was a con who wanted to be one of the

---

[1] Kill.

chaps. He got out of Rampton which was a bit of a feat in itself but, of course, they nicked him again. I had to reply and say I was sorry but I'd no idea.

So if any of you do know where Johnny is, and you want to tell me, all you've got to do is look me up on www.madfrankiefraser.co.uk